Black and
Mennonite

Black and Mennonite

A Search for Identity

Hubert L. Brown

Introduction by
Katie Funk Wiebe

Wipf and Stock Publishers
150 West Broadway • Eugene OR 97401
2001

Black and Mennonite

By Brown, Hubert L.
Copyright©1976 by Herald Press and Wipf & Stock
ISBN: 1-57910-576-9

Reprinted by *Wipf and Stock Publishers*
150 West Broadway • Eugene OR 97401

Previously published by Herald Press, 1976.

Dedicated to the two churches I've pastored,
Bethel Mennonite Church, Norristown, Pennsylvania,
and Spencer Mennonite Church, Swanton, Ohio
(in memory of Walter Hobson,
a sincere brother in Christ
who gave much to everyone he met).

CONTENTS

INTRODUCTION

I heard a strange thing the other day.

The speaker at the service said he was an Anabaptist Mennonite. That made a lot of sense to me.

But I could see plainly that he was black. And that didn't make the same kind of sense. A black Mennonite! In Africa, in a mission, it might work, but here?

Then he asked the audience the same questions that were leapfrogging through my mind: Can a person be black and Mennonite at the same time? What is a black Anabaptist Mennonite Christian? What are the implications of a white European heritage for a contemporary American black?

The speaker was Hubert Brown, black theologian from Elkhart, Indiana, on a lecture tour under the auspices of the John F. Funk Lectureship. He was speaking at several schools and churches in the Kansas area.

Brown boldly but warmly asserted his right to be an Anabaptist Mennonite. He indicated he has had a 25-year connection with the Mennonites, having been introduced to them as a young boy at a church mission near Philadelphia.

He has attended Mennonite schools such as Christopher Dock High School, Goshen College, and Mennonite Biblical Seminary. For a time he wore the plain coat. He has visited Mennonite historical points of interest in Europe, such as churches and cemeteries and statues.

He has eaten Mennonite soul food.

But all of these factors didn't make him a Mennonite. He waived aside his right to the ethnic goodies, such as *Zwieback* and *Lebkuchen*, which numerous Mennonites clasp to their bosoms and find sticking to their ribs. Instead he claimed for himself and other contemporary blacks the spiritual heritage of the Anabaptists.

This heritage, he asserted was for all men, not just the white descendants of the Anabaptists. It included the believers church concept. The Anabaptists had emphasized that Christ-followers must be a burden-bearing community, serious about caring for the oppressed in their midst. They had rejected systems of ecclesiastic hierarchies. They saw all men as equal before God. He wanted these truths for himself and all black people.

But as he spoke, I continued my monologue with myself. If a black can be a Mennonite, can a Mennonite ever be black? What are the implications of a black slave heritage for contemporary American Mennonites? It seemed as fair to ask these questions as the first ones.

But even before I had the questions fully formulated in my own mind, I could hear imaginery answers bouncing back at me. Why would anyone ever want to be black? Why should anyone even consider it?

But Brown had caught up to me in my thinking. He pointed out that the black man has always had to come over to the way of the white man. Today blacks move about in a black and white world. White people move about only in their white world. The black world never becomes a valid option for them. They don't want to be black, as some blacks have at times wanted to be white because it offers more advantages.

I recalled a poignant passage in Maya Angelou's *I Know Why the Caged Bird Sings* in which she describes her longing as a child to run in the wind with the breeze blowing through her long wavy blond curls, as the heroines in storybooks were described. But then she would put her hand up to her own black kinky hair and know that white beauty would never be her portion in life. She would always be black, and in her eyes, ugly.

But Brown had caught up with me again. As he had accepted, not the cultural, but the spiritual heritage of the Mennonites, so the Mennonites can become one community with the blacks if they accept the spiritual heritage of the blacks—a heritage of suffering and oppression. To understand oppression, whether physical or psychological, is to understand what it is to be black. To identify with another's hurt is to be black. To see their world as a valid and worthwhile community is to become black.

Can a black person become a Mennonite?

The real question seems to be whether a white Mennonite can become black.

Katie Funk Wiebe
Hillsboro, Kansas

AUTHOR'S PREFACE

The Spirit of the Lord is upon me, because he has anointed me to preach good news to the poor. He has sent me to proclaim release to the captives and recovering of sight to the blind, to set at liberty those who are oppressed, to proclaim the acceptable year of the Lord. Luke 4:18, 19.

All of us understand Christian theology in the context of our personal backgrounds. Most Mennonites have grown up in a white rural environment.

The perspective in the pages that follow is of a city black who became a Mennonite and adopted the Anabaptist tradition as my own. My purpose is to compare Anabaptist history and viewpoints with recent black theological thought and to suggest ways the two can contribute to each other.

As a Christian, I embody both black theology and Anabaptist thought. We black theology advocates believe that God is alive and at work among the poor, where there is oppression and suffering. We believe that we are in a unique position to talk about God, primarily because of where He is and where we are in history. We believe black theology is a part of God's continuing interaction with His people in the God-movement.

I am proposing that black theology and Anabaptist thought are not isolated movements, but rather part of the larger pattern of God at work in history. I believe that the theology of sixteenth-century Anabaptists has basic relevance for the renaissance in theological circles today.

In chapter one I tell my personal story and reflect on what it's like to be a black Christian in the Mennonite Church. Chapter two provides a brief analysis of contemporary black theology, noting its emergence and relevance to the black experience in white America. In chapter three I share my understanding of "our" radical Anabaptist heritage and suggest synthesizing the understandings of Anabaptism and black theology. The final chapter calls for a diunital approach to black/white relations, moving toward "a theology of the oppressed."

There are basically two approaches to any field of knowledge. One is the academic and theoretical, the other the dynamic and practical. The former deals with the dissemination of data and knowledge for its own sake, while the latter applies what has been discovered for the welfare of the individual and society. In the pages which follow I am concerned with the practical and the dynamic aspects of black consciousness and Anabaptist thought as they have influenced my life and my outlook on the church. I shall leave the area of pure scholarship to the exegetes, critics, historians, sociologists, and theologians who are specialists in their respective fields. I write primarily as a student with a pastoral concern.

It is significant that the Conrad Grebel Lectureship Committee commissioned me to prepare the content of this book as two Funk Lectures for the Mennonite Church. But it also is significant that I should be asked to give a presentation on a subject dealing with black consciousness in theological perspective. By this action I believe Mennonites are affirming the validity of this subject for intellectual inquiry, while filling a serious vacuum within the church's discussion and dialogue.

I especially want to thank C. J. Dyck of Associated Biblical Seminaries and Ed Riddick of Operation PUSH for their persistent encouragement and faith in my ability to articulate a particular approach to Anabaptism and black theology. They recognized long ago the necessity for persons to find wholeness and vision through investigation and reflection on the relevance of Christian faith in one's personal being and experience.

I am deeply grateful to the following colleagues and friends who helped illumine, clarify, and give shape to the thoughts included in this book: Willard Swartley, Atlee Beechy, Harold Bauman, John Fisher, Edward Stoltzfus, John Powell, Tony Brown, Ray Jackson, John Bender, and Kevin Jordan. Thanks to Helen Brown and Sharlene Kauffman for typing the manuscript, and to Mr. and Mrs. Chauncy Mull and Bessie Short for the use of their farms during the time of research and writing.

I also thank my wife, Helen, and our children, Donald and Leslie, for their remarkable understanding and support throughout the storm and calm of tension and release. Special appreciation is due the students of Hesston College, Eastern Mennonite College, Goshen College, Associated Biblical Seminaries, and many others with whom these lectures were shared.

This assignment has been a challenging, stimulating, and rewarding experience for me. I consider it to be an affirmation of the ongoing God-movement, for each disciple must see the relation between one's faith and one's person.   *Hubert L. Brown*

1

ON BEING BLACK IN A WHITE CHURCH

For the past two decades, blacks have been taking a new look at themselves and reexamining practically every aspect of their lives. This fact is particularly clear to me regarding theology and church life. Here one experiences a growing consciousness of the age-old tension between faith and human existence, church and society.

I would like to share with you some insights on what it means to be black in the Mennonite Church and to explore the relationships of black and white Christians today. Like most blacks, I came to a knowledge of the Christian faith mostly through white people. My acquaintance with Mennonites began some twenty-five years ago. At least that's what early records of the Mennonite summer Bible school in Norristown, Pennsylvania, indicate. Having the Brown family in the Bible school was a direct result of the missionary efforts of a motley-looking group of white, rural, German-background Mennonite churchmen.

Later I discovered from my mother that these folks first came to our community to pass out a small evangelistic periodical called *The Way.* They became aware of the large number of children in our family and the awful burden that my mother had in trying to wash, iron, cook, clothe, and feed all of us They began assisting my mother in various ways by bringing food baskets, by helping with the laundry, and by giving counsel on some of the problems our family faced. These Mennonites were always friendly and anxious to help our struggling family. Occasionally they would single us out for evangelism, expressing strong concern for our souls. They asked our parents if we could attend Sunday school with them, and it didn't take long for our parents to say yes. even though we were black Baptists by background, we had stayed home from church to avoid conflicts with the other children who would make fun of our patched-up pants and our worn-out shoes. But having thirteen children around the house on Sunday all day was a mess, and an invitation to attend church was a God-sent blessing.

And so the Mennonites picked us up in their fine station wagon each week and took us to Sunday school. We had additional contact with Mennonites through special meetings, summer camp, and an annual church outing which meant a trip to their huge farms, and plenty of food. Also, some of their members were egg vendors in the city who sold their dairy and poultry products to us at what seemed to be reasonable prices.

The First Mennonite Church of Norristown was started in the late twenties as a mission. The church was located in a racially changing neighborhood. But the Mennonites were rural folks who migrated to the city from Sunday to Sunday. I used to call them "white Russians," because they rushed in on Sunday morning and rushed out again. I was fifteen when I followed the example of some of my older brothers and sisters and joined the Mennonite Church. I accepted the Lord during a George Brunk revival meeting in the late fifties. Later, I renewed my covenant with the Lord in a fireside service at Camp Men-o-Land located in Finland, Pennsylvania, during one of our inner-city mission weeks at camp.

In 1960 I joined the Bethel Mennonite Church, which was formed during the summer of 1959 to minister to the "colored" families on the east end of town. Apparently the First Mennonite Church became a little uncomfortable with a lot of "colored" kids running around in their "nice" church, and some people could not take them any longer. The pastor of First Mennonite at that time was Markley Clemmer, a dynamic evangelist and a powerful church builder who decided to start the work in the east end. I became the first member of Bethel, and thought of myself as Markley's Timothy. By joining the local congregation, I soon discovered, I also became part of the Franconia Conference of the (Old) Mennonite Church, whatever that was supposed to mean.

In 1966, after two years of college, I became pastor of the Bethel congregation and enjoyed some of the most beautiful and painful years in my maturation process. I learned that I was only the second black person ever to have received a license to preach in the Franconia Conference, and that ten years earlier it would have been extremely difficult to obtain such credentials. Basically my relationship with Mennonites has always been good. I cannot forget, though, that some Mennonites have been almost too "nice" to me and to black folks in general. I have felt at times that I was being treated like a Christmas tree, like an object put on display. I have found myself alternately valued and then put aside in a manner often used with things rather than people.

Even though I was practically raised Mennonite, I

knew little of the church's history and tradition except for occasionally hearing names such as Menno Simons and Christopher Dock. As a new member of the Mennonite Church, I became acquainted with church practices which to some of us seemed quite strange, such as the holy kiss, the prayer veiling, and plain suits—practices which were vigorously taught and required of every person who identified with the Mennonite community. As I grew in my Christian understandings, I became more aware of some of the problems in the Mennonite Church.

It all began with a search for personal identity. My first big discovery was that I'm a *black* Mennonite. To say that I'm a black Mennonite carries a great deal of meaning for me now. But for many years I would not have identified with these words. I did not want to admit that I was black nor did I want to consider how unconsciously I had become a carbon copy of the white Mennonite world.

The black experience is a series of changes; it involves a dynamic growing process. In my early experience with Mennonites I was at what William E. Cross calls the "preencounter" stage. Cross writes,

> In the preencounter stage a person is programmed to view and think of the world as being non-Black, anti-Black, or the opposite of Black. The person's world view is dominated by Euro-American determinants. The sociological, political, cultural, and psychological conditions that result from this world view appear to be the same for both lower- and middle-class Black people. The content of the Black experience within the class system differs but the *context* is similar as both think, act, and behave in a manner that *degrades* Blackness.[1]

After the death of Martin Luther King, I entered the

second stage in my identity awareness, the stage of encounter. I began to reinterpret white America and her definitions. I discovered the concept of black consciousness whereby black people become aware of the meaning of their blackness in the context of whiteness.

This leads to stage three which Cross calls Immersion-Emersion. He writes,

> In this period the person immerses himself in the world of Blackness. everything of value must be Black or relevant to Blackness. The experience is an immersion into Blackness and a liberation from Whiteness. [2]

To know blackness is to know self. And to know self is to recognize others in relation to self and to experience acceptance and rejection in human encounters. For me to be conscious of my color means that I know what blackness is and become aware of the distinctions between blackness and whiteness. The admission that I am a black Mennonite springs from a series of changes that led me to discover who I was and to accept the beauty of being black with all that blackness means.

Since the rise of black power and its multifaceted expressions in black life, it is no longer possible to ignore the once-invisible black minority in America society. The black power movement of the sixties enabled the invisible to become visible, challenging the assumption that America embodies one community with a common destiny for all. Blacks like myself, taking their cues from black awareness writers, thinkers, and philosophers, began to call into question the American dream and the standard rhetoric about brotherhood and equality, the land of the free, and the home of the brave. Blacks like myself began to expect society to deal with us as new black persons who had no intention of becoming quietly assimilated and absorbed into the white world.

To understand the impact of black consciousness on black life it is necessary not to sidestep history. Blacks have had to discover their identity. This has involved us black folks in an investigation of our history and a reexamination of the reasons for our presence in a white racist society. This has led to a rejection of some of the concepts and realities of the white world. I was Christian before I came to this encounter with myself, but Christianity did not drive me to this point. Its inconsistencies insofar as blacks were shut out of the church did.

Like most blacks, I came to Christ through the influence of white people. At first, I did not realize that whites in America have generally related to blacks primarily from a position of assumed superiority. I discovered that whites enter the circumference of a relationship feeling that everything of value is on their side, and that blacks have nothing to offer. I did sense that whites were always extremely concerned about my soul and where my soul would be lodged after death. I came to faith believing in the goodness of whites, having received the benevolent acts of the white community (which I later came to recognize was paternalism in many instances).

And so in the Mennonite Church, as well as in white society, I've had to struggle and deal with what it means to be a black. The rise of black consciousness enabled me to see that I could no longer identify with the white man nor think of myself as being a part of his world. The rise of black consciousness made me understand that blacks are a separate people, with a separate history and separate cultures. I can affirm this today and am proud of black history and culture.

The black Christian in a predominantly white institution has to make a decision early in his or her life as to whether or not all that represents the white Christian experience will be internalized. This was the question that I faced. Indeed a great deal of what I experienced in the white church was internalized and believed by me. However, in my search for my own personal black identity, I began to question my role as a black Christian in the Mennonite Church and what that meant. I became quite discouraged about the church as I saw it, particularly how the church operated in the area of social concerns in trying to resolve the whole issue of racism. I discovered that white racism among Mennonites was not the result of a distorted theology, but of a theological illiteracy. The tragedy as I sensed it was that the church was neither what it professed to be nor what it was told it should be.

To me the church is to participate in the suffering of the oppressed in a godless world; the church is to be wide-awake with Jesus, identifying with the oppressed. As I looked about me I saw the brokenness of humanity. I, too, experienced brokenness—a loneliness, a sense of not being affirmed, of not having my history, my past, and my experiences respected and acknowledged. I was depressed by what I considered the irrelevance of the church. I began to see the church as nothing but a resolution-passing community that failed miserably in being a visible manifestation of God in the world. I saw the church as not being God's redemptive agent, but rather being an agent of American culture. The church was failing to create an atmosphere of radical obedience to Christ, failing to be all that God had intended for it to be. It seemed to me that the church was nothing but a fellowship that was more concerned about new buildings than about children who die of starvation, or of men who are killed because they happened to dream about a just society.

I wondered for a time whether I could continue to relate to the church. I had to make a decision. I remember attending a conference where Dale Brown, author of *The Christian Revolutionary*, said, "Sometimes one must leave the church in order to join the church." That statement had profound meaning for me.

I recall the times when I'd play over and over again Isaac Hayes's *Hot Butter Soul* album. In one song on it, "By the Time I Get to Phoenix," he sings about a guy who didn't want to leave his girl, but she kept doing wrong. This reminded me of how I felt in a white-oriented church. Hayes sings, "On the one hand you were good to me but on the other hand you were real cold, cold, you just kept hanging on. . . ." This is what it's like to live in both a black world and a white church.

To be a black Mennonite gives one the feeling of twoness, of being a part of the church and yet not being a part. And I'd think of the church when Hayes sang, "I hate to leave you baby, but I really, really, really must go, 'cause this heart of mine just can't take no more. I have taken all that I can stand. You should have known what you were doing to this man." Later in the song he sings, "Tear drops water beating under my chin. You can look at me and tell all the bag I'm in."

The black person in the white church discovers from

time to time the presence of the same kind of white arrogance that has been a part of Western civilization's way
of operating for centuries. Blacks have sensed arrogance
in the way the church responded to the crises in the city.
They have felt arrogance in theological seminaries—arrogance which enables whites to give, but not receive.
they have observed arrogance in decision-making regarding the future of minority social programs, development
funds, and literature projects. They have seen arrogance
in the realigning of regional and churchwide conference
committees in ways that avoid minority participation.
Political maneuvering and hierarchal politics are
ostensibly engaged in to accomplish the will of God.
When this happens, unfortunately the nonwhites get
hurt.

I'm still struggling with the church. As I look into Mennonite Church history, I discover that the present-day
Mennonite community has lost much of its historical
spiritual qualities. I realize that the sons of Menno must
seek to recover their spiritual past. I cannot identify with
their biological past, but I must be cognizant of their
ethnic experience. I must try to become acquainted with
that which I cannot understand, just as I think it will be
necessary for Mennonites to become aware of a black
past.

Many Mennonites have begun a new ethnic awareness
search. There has also been an ethnic identity search by
blacks. Blacks and those Mennonites who are engaged in
a pilgrimage to the past will find it to be freeing and in-
spirational. Black history has established an authentic
past. To draw upon C. Eric Lincoln's description of our
separate trips to North America I'd say, unlike the

Anabaptists who immigrated to escape from tyranny and to seek religious freedom, Africans came not by choice but because the last vestige of their freedom had been wiped out. The sons and daughters of Menno arrived in the new world seeking new ways to exploit the full potential of their humanity while the African came under conditions which denied even their basic humanity. The children of West Africa and the sons of Europe were destined for separate roles in the making of North America. For the white Mennonite, North America was to be a land of the free, where self-evident truths of life and liberty and the pursuit of happiness were sufficient grounds for justice. But for the African, North America was to mean years of slavery and segregation, followed by integration and more subtle racism.

Obviously we come from two different and separate streams of history. It is important for Mennonites—whites and blacks to know both histories. As I look back, I see a different history than of Mennonite forebears who were known as the "quiet in the land." I see how my own forefathers were forced to deny their African past. I see the internalization of slave master values. I see the insistence to affirm European values that were responsible for our enslavement. At worst, this meant accepting the slave conditions as ordained of God. At best, it meant that Shakespeare, Menno Simons, and Bach provided the standards of literary, theological, and musical creativity. In either case, our true African identify was denied. That's why Malcom X said, "The worst crime the white man has committed has been to teach us to hate ourselves."

This is different from standard Mennonite history,

quite different. Mennonites through America and Canada generally exhibited pride in their German, Swiss, and Dutch background and deliberately stayed out of touch with the world. As a consequence, Mennonites did not develop a positive attitude toward black folks. Mennonites in North America were involved in segregation in most of the same ways as the larger society. Some claim Mennonites identified with the oppressed black folks in their slavery. I am constantly told, although it has not been completely researched, that Mennonites held no slaves.

The black experience in North America is radically different from that of white Mennonites. Preston Williams, a noted black religious scholar, says the black experience can be conceptualized by three words: victimization, integration, and black awareness. Writes Preston Williams,

> Victimization refers to the fact that every Black person in America is injured or cheated by the conscious or unconscious notions of white superiority in the American mind and social system.
> Integration, unlike victimization, does not refer to all Blacks. It indicates that white racism is neither so consistent nor so comprehensive as to exclude all Black persons from a significant measure of participation in America's values, beliefs, or social institutions.[3]

Williams sees black awareness or black self-actualization as the concern for establishing and maintaining a sense of black identity and dignity. It is the concern on the part of the black man to know who he is. Black self-awareness comes to be determined in large measure by the black person's desire to become a fully historical person. He desires to know his cultural past, become rooted in it, and out of it make a contribution to all mankind. Since North America has completely distorted his role and place he must refreshen his understanding of black life in America. And so blacks like myself have had to come through this kind of troubled waters. The black awareness person says with James Baldwin,

> White people cannot in the generality be taken as models of how to live. Rather, the white man is himself in sore need of new standards, which will release him from his confusion and place him once again in fruitful communion with the depths of his own being. [4]

The question I then pose is how much of the church community in which I've become a part stands for all that I deeply hate in American life? I wonder if the church has become in the words of Bill Pannell, "my friend the enemy." James Juhnke stimulated my thinking with his article, "Mennonite Benevolence in Civic Identity."[5] In my estimation, Juhnke comes close to truth when he states, "Mennonites are an acculturating religious minority who have gradually taken on the characteristics of their American social and political environment." It is my belief that most Mennonites have simply allowed themselves to be absorbed into the larger society, the American culture. If Mennonites are a part of the larger American society, then they too are white-oriented.

It took me a long time to face up to the basic reality that there are two Americas, one white and one black. Albert Cleage points this out when he says,

> White America has power; it controls the economics,

the politics, the religion and all the institutional structures of America. Then there is black America which is powerless, in which black people control nothing, in which black people are oppressed. Two Americas: one white, one black[6]

It seems to me the problem does not grow out of the fact that some whites in America believe one thing and some believe another. Nor does it grow out of the fact that some are living in rural areas and that some are living in the cities. When it comes to blacks in America, it makes no difference. It makes no difference whether it's a white communist, a white alcoholic, a white middle-class politican, a white suburbanite, or a white Christian Mennonite. Their social attitudes are already conditioned as far as black people are concerned.

Irvin B. Horst a number of years ago in discussing Mennonites in an article entitled, "Mennonites and the Race Question," wrote,

> Frequently we (that is, the ethnic Mennonites) fail to appreciate the positive qualities of groups who are not of Swiss, German, or Dutch background. Our heritage may have given us the virtues of honesty, industry, and the ability to have well-painted and well-managed farms and homes, but it may also have given us a cold austerity of conviction, a lack of social grace, a hard individualism. Too seldom do we attract others from outside our circles and when we do, we rarely extend to them the full social privileges accorded an individual in our own group.[7]

Horst's statements are true for people of the Mennonite Church today. I think Merle Good's book, *Hazel's People*[8] (earlier published under the title, *Happy as the*

Grass Was Green), was an attempt to deal with that fact.

I recall a black Mennonite brother asking me if I was going to stay in the Mennonite Church. If we are serious about creating a new Christian community, a new sense of what the Anabaptist vision was all about, I told him, then I am quite serious about remaining Mennonite. I feel the same way that Little Anthony and the Imperials felt when they sang the song "Tears on My Pillow," back in the mid-fifties. One of the lines of that song says, "If we could start anew, I wouldn't hesitate." That's basically my reply. I believe that we can start anew. I've decided that for this time and for this period of history I will not engage in creative disaffiliation with the church. I feel that at this time there's a greater need for creative affiliation with the white church.

I can think of a number of reasons for remaining radically loyal to this present structure called the Mennonite Church, reasons that cause me to continue my covenant with the church. I believe the church can be renewed from within. I am committed to the younger black Mennonite brothers and sisters who are still trying to find their way in a white church maze. Perhaps more importantly, I want to continue my commitment to the church because of my link to Jesus Christ who gives life and because of the way in which He came and sacrificed His life for me. It is precisely because of my link to Jesus Christ, who loved me in the midst of my sin, who came and shared His life with me, that I want to share my life with others. I am committed to the church; I believe Jesus wants me to be committed to the church as a manifestation of my love for Him.

Never before has there been a time in my life which has

been more exciting and challenging and yet depressing and lonely as these times of creatively confronting the church. It seems hardly fitting for me simply to waste away in despair over the isolation of church. Creative affiliation, that's how black folks need to relate to the white church. Black Mennonites must see their role in the church as helping to shape and create the new community.

In my brief experience in the Mennonite Church I have discovered that some of my black brothers and sisters are still in the preencounter stage. I'm not sure why this is, but I feel it's unfortunate that they do not see the contradiction this portrays. These brothers neither embrace blackness as a concept nor black theology as a model, and in some instances they do not even identify with the word black. So we have a long way to go before we understand the beauty of who we are when we say black and the gifts that accompany that acknowledgement.

As Jesse Jackson says, "I am somebody!" We have much to offer the church. Here we are, fresh from those "nigger balconies" ready to enlarge the understanding of the descendants of those who created the balconies. Whites need to learn from us. They will need to acquire "soul" to understand our heritage and to develop ways to make our God their God, our people their people.

Together we must all consider ourselves to be a minority, trying to obey the voice of God, trying to serve God as authentic liberators of this sick racist society. As Mennonites, both black and white, we really need each other to become the kind of Christian community with the kind of identity and maturity that Jesus Christ wants us to have.

In these difficult times we need mature persons to explore the possibilities of new breakthroughs, and to help create a more hopeful and moral alternative community. The black person in the white church must possess strength and a sense of somebody-ness. Blacks must be active and effective, true to what God has done through Jesus Christ and through the black experience. They must be able to cope with the white establishment while at the same time maintaining contacts and emotional ties in the black community with serious radical involvement in the liberation struggle.

No doubt blacks will continue to experience a dual kind of existence, but this is required of us in being a part of a white institution. Whites also will need to experience a dual existence having us in their midst. they will need to be sensitive to our duality and understand that we are not the only ones who should live a dual existence. They, too, must become the inheritors of a dual existence. I agree with J. Lawrence Burkholder when he says, "The new Mennonite community should seek to perpetuate what is best in the Mennonite tradition without apology."[9] I urge the Mennonite community to take the history of blacks just as seriously as the creative protest of the sixteenth-century Reformers. Once the synthesis of the black experience and the biblical record and Anabaptist protest movements takes place, I think we will move from a preoccupation with abstraction and isolation to freeing each other to be God's twentieth-century new church movement.

As a black Mennonite, the great breakthrough for me was the emergence of black theology. Black theology helped me answer many of the perplexing "soul" questions I had raised about staying with the church and Christian faith in the face of oppression. Even though I liked what I saw in Anabaptism, it was black theology with its forceful message that related most to my contemporary paradox—the paradox of being an alien situated between the scorn and hatred of both the white and, at times, the black worlds.

For a while I struggled with not knowing how to answer many questions. Can the black man really accept the white man's interpretations of the Bible? Can the white man really read the New Testament without instinctively translating it in theology that addresses itself to the fundamental needs and aspirations of black folk? Can I continue to affirm a Mennonite theology, even though I know it does not relate to the ghetto experience, nor does it reflect the thinking of black Christians and their theologizing?

These kinds of questions posed real problems for me. And it has only been out of the experience of examining the emerging pages of black theology that I have been able to confront the realities of black life in a white denomination. In the next chapter, I examine black theology.

2

AN ANALYSIS OF BLACK THEOLOGY

Theology is our attempt to love God with our minds. We are, of course, to love Him with our hearts and souls and strength as well, so theology is not our total response to God. That total response includes prayer and worship and active concern for the neighbor. But theology is part of our response, and it involves thinking—thinking as rigorously and honestly as possible about the meaning of God for our lives. We are not entitled to stop thinking once we "believe." Only after we believe do we really start thinking.[1] —Robert McAfee Brown

In analyzing the message of black theology, I hope to place primary emphasis on understanding its relationship to the black experience, to the dominant church, and to contemporary American theology. My main purpose for writing this chapter is to help the reader gain an understanding of black theology, rather than to enter into some idle debate over its legitimacy. I write also with what James Cone describes as "a certain dark joy."[2] For in this research, as with all research, the researcher gains new knowledge and insights.

In defining black theology one could easily describe it as a counterpart of the black power movement. They have similar goals. Black power simply means the complete liberation of black people from white oppression by whatever means the black community thinks is necessary. Black power is synonomous with black self-determination. Black people take on human dignity and selfhood, rising to seize control of their own destiny. With the emergence of black power and new black consciousness in black life, it was no longer possible or useful to ignore the once invisible black presence. One of the major consequences of the 1960s was that the invisible became visible, demonstrating clearly the falsehood of the assumption that America was the great melting pot culture with a common destiny for all.

Throughout the sixties and into the early seventies new voices called into question the American dream. Capable and articulate blacks such as Malcolm X, Ron Karenga, Stokley Carmichael, Angela Davis, Martin Luther King, Jr., and many other significant historians, theologians, and sociologists of the black community forced society to deal with blacks as persons who did not see integration into white culture as a viable option. These men, through their prodding, their hopes, and their vision began to precipitate a new direction, to carve out a new humanity as defined by the forces of liberation. The most appropriate description of this new mood in the black community was the concept of black power.

The new black did not object to combining such words as "black and power," "black and theology," "black and church," "black and Christ," "black and God." The new blacks—young black university students, young black preachers, seminarians, and other contemporaries of mine—were neither shocked nor discouraged about the term black power. To us, the term meant black consciousness and solidarity. It meant black people controlling black people's lives, black people's economic, political, and social order. Black power meant a repudiation of the American cultural religion, a repudiation of an Americanized Christ. It meant a search for roots, a discovery of our past. It meant control of our own future.

The question for us was how to correlate Christian faith with the black liberation movement. A black theology was needed that would take into account the experience and sufferings of black people. A theology that would be ture to the biblical witness but also would know something of the meaning and significance of being a poor man in a rich, hostile, white society. For years blacks had studied in white seminaries and in white institutions. Of those blacks who probed for a theological education in white seminaries, Bishop Joseph Johnson says this,

> The black seminarians took both the theological milk and meat and even when they had consumed these, their souls were still empty. [3]

He further writes,

> Those of us who went through the white seminaries did not understand why then. We had passed the courses in the four major fields of studies; we knew Barth, Brunner, and Niebuhr. We had entered deeply into a serious study of Bonhoffer and Tillich, but we discovered that these white theologians had described the substance and had elucidated a contemporary faith for the white man. These white scholars knew nothing about the black experience, and to many of them this black experience was illegitimate and inauthentic. [4]

With such reasoning and understanding the black theology movement was born. This movement occurred during the black power, black consciousness era. Some have said that it can be described as a theological dimension of the black revolution.

James Cone, one of the leading proponents of this new theology, and author of the book, *Black Theology and Black Power*, defined it this way,

> Black theology is that theology which arises out of the need to articulate the significance of black presence in a hostile white world. It is black people reflecting religiously on the black experience. Attempting to define the relevance of the Christian gospel for their lives.[5]

While it is true that many black theologians and black scholars are indebted in a measure to white theologians and have gained many perspectives from them, it is also true that white theologians in their interpretation of the Christian faith completely ignored the black experience. The omission of black Christian experience by white theologians and churchmen meant that the message had nothing significant to say to blacks. Blacks struggling for identity and dignity were forced to look at the black Christian experience and to involve themselves in the task of making that experience applicable to the biblical past. Cornish R. Rodgers, associate editor of the *Christian Century* magazine, once wrote,

> It has been said that it is passions that give rise to ideas and not the other way around. If that is so then it must have been the miracle compassion surrounding the civil rights black power movement of the past decade that produced the heat of the blossoming forth of the exotic and powerful theology of the black experience. What is surprising, however, is that it took so long for black

imagination to begin to fashion a rigorous, systematic theology based on the peculiar torturous experiences of the black people in this country. After all, theology is merely a description of God gleaned from his mighty acts on behalf of a people.[6]

J. Deotis Roberts, in his book, *Liberation and Reconciliation: A Black Theology*, observes,

Theology is God-talk. The word "theology" is derived from two Greek words: theos, which means "God" and logos which means "reasoning" or "thinking." Thus theology is "reasoning about God."[7]

This definition has validity and in utilizing it we can agree when Robert McAfee Brown says, "Theology is our attempt to love God with our minds." Joseph Washington, black religionist says,

The task of a theologian is to discover what God is doing in the world and to rally around to further His intention.[8]

If we accept these two definitions as a basis for defining theology then we can easily understand James Cone's definition of black theology. Theology entails a balance between the dimensions of a personal or inclusive reality, and of a universal or a global reality. The message of the gospel must be clothed in a situational context. For black theology, this context is the oppressed community. As James Cone says in his first book, "Black theology is a theology of the black community."[9] Major Jones in his book, *Black Awareness: A Theology of Hope*, writes,

In a true sense then, black theology, like all theology,

arises out of a people's common experiences with God. At this moment in history, the black community seeks to express itself theologically from a black frame of reference in language that speaks to the current condition of black people.[10]

Cone further writes,

A black theologian wants to know what the gospel has to say to a man who is jobless and cannot get work to support his family because the society is unjust. He wants to know what God's word is to the countless black boys and girls who are fatherless and motherless because white society decreed that blacks have no rights. Unless there is a word from Christ to the helpless then why should they respond?[11]

It is clear from this perspective of black theology that we can see a direct fusion of the Christian faith to the existential conditions, the situational context under which blacks live and have their being. And so the task of theologizing requires an understanding of a anthropological orientation as well as the environment of blacks. Geddes Hanson of Princeton rightly says,

Black theology . . . is a self-conscious effort to relate the experience of American blackness to the corpus of Christian theology. Proceeding from the conviction that theology itself is an attempt to deal with the realities of human experience from the perspective of divine-human negotiations, black theology lifts up the reality of the experience of blackness in America as being relevant to the theological task.[12]

Major Jones writes that,

Black theology differs from traditional theology by the simple reason that it may not be as concerned to describe such traditional things as the eternal nature of God's existence as it is to deal with the impermanent, paradoxical, and problematic nature of human existence. Much of the task of black theology is to reclaim a people from humilitation and in the process of doing it may well neglect such unrelated subjects as humility before man and guilt before God. If black theology is to speak realistically and cogently to a people whose lives have been worn down, whose best hopes have so often been frustrated, and who have been reminded at every turn by human word and action that they are less worthy of so much of what ordinary humans possess, it must have a new and fresh message of hope for the future.[13]

This theology of the black experience is an outgrowth of the black power movement beginning with the sixties. Black theology is a theological response to the crisis precipitated by the black revolution of the past decade. Black theology is a dynamic reflection upon black religious experience indicating that it has significance and deserves to be examined and understood. Black theology emancipates, it breaks the shackles, it lets the oppressed go free.

As I deal with black theology, I find that it has two main poles—liberation and reconciliation. These are suggested by J. Deotis Roberts in his book, *Liberation and Reconciliation: A Black Theology.* The Commission on Theology of the National Committee of Black Churchmen in a statement on black theology, said,

For us, Black theology is the theology of black liberation. It seeks to plumb the black condition in the light of

God's revelation in Jesus Christ so that the black community can see the gospel is commensurate with the
achievement of black humanity. Black theology is a
theology of "blackness." It is the affirmation of black humanity that emancipates black people from white racism
thus providing authentic freedom for both white and black
people. It affirms the humanity of white people in that it
says "No" to the encroachment of white oppression.[14]

In saying that liberation represents one of the main
poles of black theology, we see God as being identified
with the liberation of the oppressed from earthly bond-
age. And this grows out of the biblical view of divine
revelation. The biblical God is involved in the historical
process. He participates in human events to liberate His
people. In black theology the theme of liberation is traced
through the Old Testament. Throughout Israelite history,
God acts to liberate Israel. The meaning of the exodus
from Egypt, the covenant at Sinai, the conquest and set-
tlement of Palestine, the united kingdom and its division,
the rise of great prophets, and the exodus from Babylon—
these all reveal God's mighty acts, God delivering His
people from tyranny and from peril. They show God at
work releasing the oppressed from the oppressors.

Black theology follows this theme through the New
Testament. Jesus Christ, the incarnate One, takes upon
Himself the oppressed condition so that all men may be
what God created them to be. Jesus is the Liberator. He
announces His intentions in Luke 4:18, 19. He went
about preaching the good news of liberation, releasing
those who had been hooked by the oppressors of their
day. Black theology proclaims the message of Galatians
5:1, "For freedom in Christ has set us free."

What does all of this have to say about our present condition? In essence, this gospel revealed in the biblical past is a gospel of liberation. The same God is at work today active on behalf of the oppressed.

In America God is at work releasing the oppressed in the black community. Black theology sees God as He is revealed in the struggle for black liberation. It sees the symbolic relationship between a black oppressed presence in North America and the oppressed people in the biblical past. This then is one revolutionary dimension in our thinking and reasoning about God. James Cone rightly asserts

> that no white theologian has ever taken the oppression of black people as a point of departure for analyzing God's activity in contemporary America.[15]

This particular task seems to have been left to those persons who have caught a new and a fresh glimpse of God's work, a vision of what God has been trying to say through the experiences of the past several decades in this society and indeed throughout black history.

Bishop Johnson notes that what we have learned about Jesus as interpreted and expounded by white American theologians is severely limiting. He says,

> This is due to the simple reason that these white scholars have never been lowered into the murky depth of the black experience of reality. they never conceived the black Jesus walking the dark streets of the ghettos of the North and the sharecropper's farm in the Deep South without a job, busted, and emasculated. These white theologians could never hear the voice of Jesus speaking in the dialect

of Blacks from the southern farms, or in the idiom of the Blacks of the ghetto. This severe limitation of the white theologians' inability to articulate the full meaning of the Christian faith has given rise to the development of black theology. [16]

What happens to the person who is exposed to black theology? Major Jones gives a positive view of what happens when a black person honestly confronts the concept of black theology. Jones writes,

> Black theology then may well become that truth which places a black person for the first time in touch with a deep core of self which is the real. And once a man finds such a self he is prepared to give all for it. This is the liberating intent of black theology. [17]

Jones makes sense to me on this subject yet many people question, why a *black* theology? Why is it referred to as black? Bishop Johnson explains,

> The difficulties which most people have with the phrase black theology is conditioned by their understanding of the word black. The rejection of blackness is so deeply rooted in the black man's experience in this nation that anything associated with the term black provokes a negativism, a refusal which is instantaneous and final. To these black scholars, or they may prefer to be called scholars, the word black has a sinister meaning. For them, the term black means evil, erroneous, devilish, malicious, suspicious, crafty, ignorant, sinful, and ugly. Blackness for many Negroes is a symbol for that which this American culture seeks to destroy and therefore it has no place in a society which is dominated by the concept white or whiteness. [18]

He further writes,

> Some black and white scholars deny the legitimacy of a
> black theological discipline but readily embrace German
> theology. When black and white scholars are asked why
> they embrace German theology they answer readily that
> the German scholars have a definite methodology, canons,
> criteria, and approaches and that the Germans' experience
> provides the milieu or the fellowship out of which all
> German theology emerges. These scholars point with
> pride to the works of Schleiermacher, Ritschl, and Har-
> nack. They are informed and stimulated by the works in
> New Testament of such German scholars as Bultmann and
> Bornkamn. Further, these scholars admit also that there is
> "white American theology," and they insist that there are
> several traditions or histories which have shaped white
> American theological thought: the tradition of supernatu-
> ralism, the tradition of idealism, the tradition of
> romanticism, the tradition of naturalism, and the tradition
> of existentialism. [19]

He says,

> The black and white scholars who repudiate the concept
> of black theology embrace the theologies which have
> arisen out of other racial Christian experiences. [20]

These blacks and others are unfortunately uneman-
cipated. To be sure the theology that arises out of the
black Christian experience is Christian, Christ-centered.
It is also black. It is a theology that grows out of the black
community's experiences with God.

Also, as we mentioned earlier, the dynamics of the
black awareness movement fostered reexaminations and
redefinitions for the blacks, creating new black consciousness and a new understanding of the Christian faith. Ever

since the emergence of black awareness, black expression
has appeared quite diversified—diversified in the sense
that it was labeled radical or militant, revolutionary or
reactionary. This was true in the theological realm as well
as with the underlying unity of black religious thought
being based on the black experience. This black
experience can be conceptualized by the three typologies
of Preston Williams referred to earlier—victimization, integration, and black awareness.

Carlton L. Lee, in an article entitled "Toward a Sociology of the Black Religious Experience," says that,
"James Cone has articulated effectively a militant or
radical theology of a black religious experience."[21] Lee
goes on to say that,

> The accommodative or concilatory principle is
> presented in the stance of Major J. Jones. Dr. Jones
> belongs to the liberal tradition of his denomination with a
> perspective that may be colored by his fairly longtime role
> in the bureaucracy of a highly structured organization. He
> is almost conservative.[22]

There appears to be a wide spectrum of black theological
thought. Albert B. Cleague, Jr., the pastor of the Shrine of
the Black Madonna Church, represents a black Christian
nationalism revolutionary perspective of black theology.
Another outstanding black theologian is J. Deotis Roberts
whose book, *Liberation and Reconciliation: A Black
Theology*, was referred to earlier. Roberts seeks to reconcile the radical view of James Cone with a much more
moderate black theology. Other moderate black theologians include Joseph Washington, Preston Williams,
Geddes Hanson, and Miles Jones. Vincent Harding has

articulated well the theology of the black power re-
ligionists along with Bishop Joseph A. Johnson who is
among the contemporary proponents of black theology.

Black Theology and the Church

Keep in mind that any criticism I may make of the
church is tempered with feelings that the church has been
very meaningful to me. I'm not sure what would have
happened to me had it not been for the caring and sharing
ministry of so many sisters and brothers in the church. I
have benefited from the teaching, preaching, and healing
ministries within the church. The influence of church in
my life and the continuation of God's grace which
transforms individuals enable me to say that I am committed to the church. I am committed to the kingdom. I
am committed to the gospel and lifestyle of Jesus Christ
which seek to bestow abundant life upon all who would
respond. Yet I have a deep concern for the church and for
the direction it may be heading. This concern grows out
of my love and commitment for the church.

At one point in my life, I had given up on the church
because I felt the church was unresponsive to the needs of
the oppressed. And even today, in the midst of renewal,
the church still maintains an insensitivity and a coldness
toward the problems and concerns of minority folks.
When one talks of the matter of a personal relationship to
God, the church has been meaningful and has offered a
great deal. On the issues of peace and nonresistance and
the free church tradition, the church has helped me
greatly. But when it comes to social issues, it seems to me
the church falls far short of seeing her role as participating
with God concretely and positively in bringing about

peace on earth and goodwill toward men and women. I know this from the experience of being a black person in America and a black in the Mennonite Church.

Historically, while blacks were being exploited in every way possible Mennonites simply enjoyed life down on the farm and played it cool. Our church had become introverted, interested primarily in preservation. And somehow that philosophy carried over into the battle for human rights. rather than stepping out into the open against injustices to blacks, our church maintained a refrigerator-type relationship, continuing its noninvolvement tradition. Our church stood by and witnessed the inhumane treatment of black people for some 350 years. Our church allowed the disease of segregation to shape her thinking, and her isolation became more complete. Our church not only permitted segregation to become her pattern of life, she allowed it to dominate America. Our church adopted a middle-class way of life with a middle-class way of thinking.

Unfortunately, the Mennonite Church has failed miserably in being a radical manifestation of God at work in the world. We have failed in creating an atmosphere of the first- and sixteenth-century protest. Particularly, we have failed to bring about radical obedience to Christ which was evident in the sixteenth-century Anabaptist thrust. Down through the years and even to the present moment, our church developed and maintained a superiority complex, a white-only attitude. This has created an establishment of Sunday morning status quo dwellers, persons who have failed to grasp the full meaning of the gift of salvation, persons who have failed to take part in the activity and movement of God in the world.

Mennonite theological thought has refused to take seriously the black liberation movement. Although the black quest for liberation can hardly be ignored, yet Mennonite theological thought has managed to do so. It has remained independent of black identity. It has remained silent regarding the place of the black man in American society. Unfortunately, within the whole of the North American church there has been a marriage of American theologians to the structures of society.

Few American theologians identify with the oppression of blacks in America. In Mennonite circles little action has taken place within the seminaries and the colleges in responding affirmatively to the crises of black people. Only a few of our institutions offer courses dealing with blacks and have hired black professional personnel on their faculties, and even this came about only after much agitation. The fact that the percentage has been so infinitesimal gives support to the racist assumption that blacks are unimportant.

Much of the dilemma of which I am speaking can be attributed to the church's failure to deal in a positive manner with the nature of God in society. It is unfortunate that the church has not maintained an awareness of God's activity in human history. It has not drawn attention to the fact that God loves His creation. He nurtures His children and brings their straying feet back to Himself. And God, who breaks the power of cultural idols, can put all of us once again in touch with His life. The church has had problems differentiating between the God of the Old Testament and the God of culture. The God who constantly speaks to humanity. The God who constantly seeks to fulfill His creation in us. The God who comes to us and lives among us. The God who seeks to find us as He did the nobodies who became the people of Israel as recorded in Exodus 19:4.

There are times when I do believe the Mennonite Church seriously tried to hear the voice of God and respond to God's call.

I believe that in developing the resolution of 1955, "The Way of Love in Christian Race Relations," there was a clear indication of God at work. I believe the agony and frustration which precipitated the establishment of the Minority Ministries Council was a time when God was speaking. I believe those sincere and honest persons who, out of deep-seated and earnest listening to God, responded voluntarily to monies for the Compassion Fund signaled again that God's people were listening to Him. But unfortunately the majority of Mennonites in the pew kept isolated from this kind of mission. They were not only detached but in quiet, bitter and violent opposition to the goals and aspirations of this type of community of faith. It seems to me that the church is on the brink of a life-and-death struggle, in terms of whether or not it can be a useful institution in precipitating social change.

If only we would stop long enough to listen. I feel deeply that God is speaking to Christian America today. He is in communication with those persons who have decided to follow Him, really to follow Him. The road behind them is the cross before them, no turning back, no turning back. To those persons God has stirred up issues of concern—priorities. Among these priorities are minority concerns, the issue of peace, the separation of church and state, the reverence and value of human life, and respect for our environment. Young people like myself have made these some of the major concerns for today and yet those who have controlled the church place these issues very low in their priority for the church. They have drowned out minority concerns with cries for quietism, God and country talk, and for deciding what color toilet tissue to buy for the church rest rooms. They seem to ignore the issue of God-intervention in this problematic twentieth century.

Many times those who sit in power refuse to hear the voice of God coming through the young, the Chicano, the Indian, and the black. They refuse the voice that seeks to challenge the failure of the church to make black and white reconciliation more of an imperative than reorganization and window-dresssing experimentation which seeks to ostracize minorities from the total decision-making aspects of church life. They refuse the voice that seeks to challenge the myth of white power and privilege that has provided administrative posts in our denomination, deanships in our theological institutions, secretaryships awarded on the basis of whether or not a person has white skin rather than ability and call. This dissident voice seeks to challenge the insensitivity of the white majority concerning its use of power, the insensitivity that alienates and polarizes minority-majority relations.

Thus the rise of a black theology. Black theology comes to remind us that the judgment of God is upon us as we overlook the moral and theological basis of human relations and social responsibility. Black theology suggests that human life can become more human only when permitted to accept a personhood that is of birth. Black theology leads us to the theological conference table and offers an evaluation, a judgment which might help the church come to itself, and thereby, like the prodigal son, return to the Father and find new blessing, new vitality, and new relationship.

John Powell, former executive secretary of Minority Ministries Council for the Mennonite Church in a paper entitled "Toward a Unified Black Theology," writes,

> To understand the dynamics of black theology, both in America and Africa, is to understand the uniqueness of the way black people see themselves related to each other, and to God. The black church has always seen God in the midst of them. [23]

This is so true. They had met God. They saw Him. They were baptized by Him, and they became identified with Him. In times of trial and tribulation God was the ever present companion to pick up the lonely and the tired. God made life and the endurance of oppression a bit more tolerable. Paul Lawrence Dunbar expressed it quite well when he wrote,

> When storms arise/And dark'ning skies/About me threatning lower,/To thee, Lord, I raise mine eyes/To thee my tortured spirit flies/For solace in that hour./Thy mighty arm/Will let no harm/Come near me nor befall me;/Thy voice shall quiet my alarm,/When life's great battle waxeth warm—/No foeman shall appall me./Upon thy breast/Secure I rest/From sorrow and vexation;/No more by sinful care oppressed/But in thy presence ever blest,/Oh God of my salvation. [24]

One gets the sense of final security, freedom from sorrow, protection from sin. This is achieved because my life is in

God's hand. "It seems clear," Benjamin Mays said, "that God is an instrument of escape from the hard, unpleasant realities of this life."[25] The black church developed a sophisticated awareness of God's intervention and God's interaction in times of acute distress. The black Christian generally assumed that God existed. His concern was, Does God care? Is God just, loving, and merciful? Is God all-powerful? Is God near? Does He watch over me? One did not doubt the goodness of God. As Charles S. Johnson writes, "The one cardinal sin was doubt. Doubt that there was a God and that He was good."

Within the black church experience the Spirit of God Himself broke forth into the lives of the people, building them up where they were torn down. And propping them up on every leaning side. God's presence was with His people and His will provided them with the courage and the strength to make it through. If they would only hold out, He would get them over to the other side. In theological terminology the God of Abraham, Isaac, and Jacob was a living God, a God who was present in times of trouble (Psalm 46:1). J. Deotis Roberts said,

> It is rather easy to understand why black slaves and their descendants have found comfort and assurance in the Old Testament. The witness and activity of the Holy Spirit as seen in the New Testament can be of equal inspiration to the black Christians. The Holy Spirit of God dwelling within the new Israel, the church, is life-giver, comforter, guide and strengthener.[26]

Down through the years black folks reflected the nature and providence of God as an escape from the shame, the myth, projected on them by a sick society. A good example of this was Robert Russa Moton, former principal of the Tuskegee Institute, and the successor to Booker T. Washington. Benjamin Mays writes of Moton's statement,

> The idea that the Negro is God's most perfect handiwork is taken from a speech delivered at Memorial Meeting in honor of Booker T. Washington, held in New York City, February 11, 1916. Moton asserts so strongly that Negroes are just as good as other people and that it is disastrous to the fullest development of the race for them to believe that they are inferior and accursed of God, that he virtually accuses God of being partial to the Negro.[27]

Moton's exact words were,

> If any of us, because of weaknesses and failings within our race, or because of unfairness, injustice, and inconvenience without, or because of the color of our faces and the texture of our hair, have been hitherto lacking in appreciation of our race, or have been afraid to be unmistakably identified with the Negro race, let us, in the name of the God who made us, forever dispel any such foolish, childish, disastrous notions. Let us remember, once and for always, that no race that is ashamed of itself, no race that does not respect, honor, and love itself, can gain the confidence and respect of other races or will ever be truly great and useful.
>
> Let us remember, also, that we are not an accursed people; that races with whiter faces have, and are still going through difficulties infinitely more trying and embarrassing than much that faces us; that we have in this country vast opportunities for growth and development, as well as for usefulness and service. We are creatures of God's most perfect handiwork, and any lack of appreciation on our part is a reflection on the great Creator. Though we Negroes are black, and though we are living

under hampering difficulties and inconveniences, God meant that we should be just as honest, just as industrious, just as skillful, just as pure, just as intelligent, just as God-like, as any human beings that walk on the face of God's earth.[28]

In our modern setting, black theologians see God as one who has stirred up the black community to a sense of pride and liberation. The black church's view of God is related to the doctrine of providence—affirming, asserting that God cares. "He's a rock in a weary land, a shelter in a mighty storm." He knows all our needs and He will provide. He fights our battle. He protects us from physical danger, sickness, and disease, if our ways are pleasing to Him. "All things work together for good to them that love God." God is just and He will bring slaveholders to the judgment seat. God will come conquering. God carries on the work of liberation. He helps us in the complete emancipation of the ungodly influences of a racism that divides us from our fellowman. This is how God is viewed in black theology. And this is how God is viewed in black church doctrines.

God is a wheel in the middle of the wheel. He's my rock, my sword, my shield. The black church that developed in the pre-civil war days learned of this God, and gave theological interpretation which far outdistanced white understanding and the white person's ability to grasp what was being said. For black folks, as J. E. Lowery, Chairman of SCCC said, "The early black church fused their existential situation with their theological situation without the phraseology." They fused it with their situation in slavery. And to paraphrase J. E. Lowery,

They probably, after listening to a white sermon during those slave days, walked down the hillside to a shady tree and started the first plantation seminary. And there they began to throw together in their own style and through their own form of hermeneutics that which they had picked up from the back of the white congregation. And so you had one fellow saying, "heaven," and the dean of the school probably said, "everybody talking about heaven ain't going there," and one of the faculty probably said, "shoes" and another one said "I have shoes, all God's children have shoes and when we get to heaven we going put on our shoes, we're going walk all over God's heaven."[29]

To the black persons, shoes symbolized acceptance into the household, the actual acceptance into the forever family of God. And with shoes on the feet one can walk, jump, run all over God's heaven. One can be jubilant and rejoice. It was in this pre-civil war situation that black theology was born. While the name black theology was not used, the black church began to associate God with their own needs. They saw God as that one who was moving in their midst, delivering them from oppression. Black theology, like black power, was born out of failure of the white world to relate to the needs of the oppressed--out of the failure of the white theological world to relate the biblical reality of our faith to the existential condition of where we live.

The same can be said concerning black interpretations of Jesus. J. D. Lowery further cites the example of slaves singing "Steal Away to Jesus." To steal away to Jesus meant hiding under some hay on a wagon bound for the promised land of the North. To steal away to Jesus meant leaving the old plantation at midnight with the stars as my guide and with Harriet Tubman to find my way out of oppression. So in a real sense the Jesus of the pre-civil war days was synonymous with freedom and justice. The Jesus black folks came to know was the Son of God, whose mission and activity was to liberate from oppression. God called upon His Old Testament people to see the connection between His deliverance and His activity in the world. His prophets speak of it. When Jesus came, He took His cues from the prophet Isaiah in announcing His mission to the Jews. He proclaimed that God's new thing was with the oppressed as recorded in Luke 4:18,19.

It is interesting to note that Christ was born among the poor. In Christ's baptism, He announces that the coming of the kingdom is to be for the poor. In His temptation He makes clear to His adversary that He will not be diverted from His work to the poor and oppressed. Satan did not have the power to redirect God's will for His Son. The reality of Christ's work was one of liberation. At the heart of Christ's ministry is His commitment to the traitors, the adulterers, the sinners, and even to the despised Samaritans, the oppressed.

The black church saw Jesus as the oppressed one and they understood His way. They sought to identify with Him. In Him they would find freedom. His death and resurrection were viewed as the revelation of the freedom of God. Christian freedom is to recognize the conquering of death by Christ. Man no longer has to be afraid of dying. Martin Luther King, Jr., in his last public address, spoke of having been on the mountain. He said that he knew that the threat of death was stalking him. However, he added, "I'm not fearing no man, for mine eyes have seen the glory of the coming of the Lord." Moments later his throat was splattered over the motel balcony. The death of Christ in black theological thought is identified as freedom—a freedom to say "no" to the oppressor in spite of the threat of death.

Black theology seeks to interpret the significance of the resurrected Christ in terms of the black experience. Theology is never content with merely studying the being of Christ. His activity, His deliverance, and His resurrection are all bound together and analyzed through the eyes and ears of one's experience with Him. The church must become aware of the theological consciousness on the part of blacks as blacks seek to analyze the gospel of Jesus Christ in the light of an oppressed situation. Most assuredly, we believe God is at work. God is powerful. He is unleashing His power so that full appreciation of His lordship and radical hearing of Him can proceed.

Violence and Reconciliation

I hope we will not to confuse misconceptions of black power associated with violence with the authentic interpretation of the Christian mission and the Christian gospel in black theology. Unfortunately, many people tend to associate black with violence. While this is sometimes done deliberately to confuse, it is nonetheless to be rejected. Black theology, as I perceive it, does not seek to place on its theological ladder a rung of violence. While violence may be part of some theological statements by so-called radical black theologians, it's not a part of black theology as such. One must understand, however, that there are two clashing ideologies: the ideology of the oppressed and the ideology of the oppressor. Black theology rejects the kind of American ideological morality which seeks to affirm all violence on the part of the dominant society or the oppressor, and condemns any violence on the part of the oppressed. Black theology rejects behavior and attitudes which seek to precipitate hostility and division between races.

I define violence as any violation of the basic human rights of a person, be they social, economic, moral, or political. These rights of man form a complex whole which cannot be separated without doing fundamental violence. An example of this is the imposition of censorship by government. When we look at it carefully and clearly, censorship is a violation of my quest for truth. I live under the illusion of a falsehood without it. Therefore, the government has deprived me. It has impeded by search. This impediment is intolerable to me, a rational, thinking human being. It is a violence to me in the most profound way.

Now violence can be exercised in both a covert and overt fashion. It can be social violence as well as individual violence. It can be mass violence against persons and property as happens in riots, or a deed against individuals. But as a manifestation of rage against the prevailing and offensive social, economic, and political order, which has already done massive violence to the fundamental rights that are granted to each person under the United States constitution, it has new and different meanings. I see black theology as condemning the kind of American mentality that wants to lock up those who throw bricks in ghettos, but completely ignores the violence of absentee landlords, who charge scandalous prices for run-down, rat-infested, below-standard housing. It is clear that black theology condemns the exploitation of swindlers who squeeze every cent they can out of poor people through their loan agencies and organizations by trickery and by small print in illegal contracts. This kind of violence we cannot ignore, we cannot bless, we cannot sanction.

Neither can we sanction the kind of violence that we find in our church political hierarchy, that keeps promoting white folk into decision-making positions of power with no regard to race, color, or creed. It seems to me that it is time for personnel officers and those untitled church recruiters to begin seeking staff persons with due regard to race, color, and creed. For too long time the church has operated under the principle of no due regard to race and that no due regard has usually meant no minority persons. That is institutional violence.

Black theology condemns the violence of self-deception. Black theology condemns the violence of mistrust, the violence of racial hatred. The roots of violence here are deep, precisely because they have the nodules of racism attached to them. The very notion of the humanity of a person and his right to free movement in society is shattered. Such violence turns whole groups of men into things. Black theology condemns the violence of the mass media and commercial interests that seek to brainwash people by saying it was black who did this, who robbed that. There is a strong negation of black in some of our most prominent communication media.

In black theology the question is raised, "How do you respond to the evil and violence that is ingrained in our present system?" The real issue is what choice the Christian makes between the potential violence of the black community and the continued violence of the system.

Must the Christian choose the lesser evil? Vincent Harding says, "We cannot escape such questions by saying we do not believe in violence when we participate in 'the violence of the status quo.' " From my theological frame of reference I reject violence for two reasons. First, as J. E. Lowery has said, it is self-defeating; and second, my roots in Christ are deep and my church history now extends to the life of the Anabaptists in the sixteenth century.

But no one can disapprove the fact that the black community has been preconditioned toward violence by the white community. This preconditioning has taken place historically in the black community because that community has been treated with the Richard Nixon syndrome of "benign neglect." Through years of neglect, through years of being invisible, an entire community rises up out of the valley of despair to one last glimpse of hope. The hope is, I'll break these chains someway.

Black theology rejects the kind of violence that asks blacks to respect law and order while being shafted on every side, for we know that "law" means keeping blacks in their place for "order." Black theology seeks to introduce and address itself to the issue of reconciliation, however, not on white folks' terms, but in the terms of the oppressed. Years of integration have taught black folks a lesson that whenever we are not there to define, white folks misconstrue the conceptions, be it good or bad, of what coming together and brotherhood is all about. This was done cleverly and systematically in the area of integration talk.

For the white mind integration meant the movement of every institution, every corporate pattern from black to white so that my old childhood descriptive slogan became quite true, "If you're white, you're all right, if you're brown stick around, if you're black get back." Everything in the white world was good and glorious and black folks were called upon to deny their own being—to hug, grasp, and acclaim white folks, to sing "We are one in the spirit, we are one in the Lord" without ever feeling like two had become one; rather, one had absorbed the other. J. Deotis Roberts said,

> I do not advocate integration as a goal. Integration is a goal set by whites and is still based upon the superordination/subordination principle of whites over blacks, even blacks with superior education and experience to whites under whom they must live and serve. In any situation where whites write the agenda for integration whether in government, business, education, industry, land, or religion, this is what integration means. The slave-master, servant-boss, inferior-superior mentality underlies all the integration schemes in which whites write the agenda. This is the reason why I am against integration.[30]

In black theology our blackness is not to be turned to whiteness. To us integration does not mean that everything should move from blackness to whiteness but from wrong to right. It was white theology that was in the forefront promoting the moving from black to white. Everything! So that blacks could not positively appreciate their own heritage, consider their own worth. While I am basically opposed to separatism, I believe as Leon Watts states, that,

> If ever there will be a merger, the only merger of black and white institutions will be when blacks have developed their own institutions and whites have overcome the superordination complex, only then can we begin to move to a

position of equalization out of which proper white/black reconciliation can take place.[31]

My friend Bill Pannell says that "one of the frustrations in black America has been our inability to make white America hear us." The "us" he is referring to is the young and the disinherited who have been turned on by religion but turned off by the church. We who are interested in the church grappling with the social order. We who are interested in seeing the church break out of its whitewashed sepulchers and move with the stream of God's activity in history. If only you would listen, if only you could hear the voice of God riding on the gift of blackness, riding on the gift of those who have sprung out of their "nigger balconies" or "Negro pews" to raise their voice in articulation of a new kind of theology that springs from the depth of where we are, that deals with the depths of where we must go. James Baldwin, in writing to his nephew, says to us,

> These men are your brothers, your lost younger brothers and if the word integration means anything, this is what it means. That we with love shall force our brothers to see themselves as they are, to cease fleeing from reality and begin to change it. For this is your home my friend. Do not be driven from it. Great men have done great things here and will again and we can make America what America must become. It will be hard, James, but you come from sturdy peasant stock, men who picked cotton, dammed rivers, and built railroads and in the teeth of the most terrifying odds achieved an unassailable and monumental dignity.[32]

He closed his letter to his nephew James by saying, "We

cannot be free until they are free." And so, this leads us to the issue of our mission and hope, and I think that my hope is summed up in what James Baldwin is saying, "Forcing, prodding my brothers to see the reality and to change it," recognizing that I cannot be liberated until we together are liberated.

Black people are hopeful that God will remain faithful as He was in the past, that God will continue to move in history, delivering and liberating the oppressed. We are hopeful that the future will yield fruit, because God's Word to us is that we shall reap what we sow. And so, with our backs bent as in the years of our own forefathers we continue to stretch forth our hands, planting the seed of reconciliation, planting the seed of repentance, planting the seed of love and hope. We pray to God that we will reap a harvest of brotherhood based not upon laws and legal systems, but based upon a dynamic awareness of God's pulling us and bringing us together, black and white, into His kingdom of social leveling where He will wipe away all tears from our eyes, where there will be no pain and suffering, where the former things will have passed away, where the old will have become new. Joy lies on the morning horizon.

Well, this may sound a bit idealistic, but it is not impractical, for we are on the brink of totally demolishing and liquidating ourselves or of totally accepting each other. As Whitney Young said, "Either we will live together as brothers or we will die together as fools." Again, the emergence of black theology and black awareness can be summed up as one of the great breakthroughs of our present age.

The special significance of black theology to me is that

it helped me to reflect upon the meaning and presence of God in my life in the context of being black in white hostile society, and as a part of a white church. In the next chapter, I analyze my understanding and attitude toward the history and heritage of the Mennonite Church and its relationship to me, a black.

3

AN ANALYSIS OF ANABAPTISM

My purpose in this chapter is to consider how I as a
minority black person relate to Anabaptist theology. Isaac
Sackey of Ghana in an address to the AFRAM Conference
held in Kenya, East Africa, said, "We need to explore the
Scriptures prayerfully and determine the best Anabaptism can offer for the world in general and black people in
particular." Who are the Anabaptists? Walter Klaassen,
Canadian Mennonite and author of the book, *Anabaptism: Neither Catholic Nor Protestant*, writes,

> Anabaptist was the nickname given to a group of Chris-
> tians in the sixteenth century. It simply meant one who bap-
> tizes again. A person could not be called a dirtier name in
> sixteenth-century Christian Europe. By its enemies, Ana-
> baptism was regarded as a dangerous movement—a
> program for the violent destruction of Europe's religious and
> social institutions. Its practices were regarded as odd and
> anti-social: its beliefs as devil-inspired heresy.[1]

I am interested in analyzing the message of the
Anabaptists for several reasons. First, the present-day
Mennonites, of which I am a part, trace their origins
directly to the Anabaptists. Second, as Franklin Littell
has suggested, "out of the experience of the Anabaptist
counter-culture, certain lessons emerged which apply

well to the world at large." And third, an understanding of Anabaptism may help in formulating a relevant theology that can speak to life in contemporary North America, as an oppressed minority. My interest in Anabaptism grows out of my association in the Mennonite Church with some of its historians, theologians, and researchers. New books, plays, and many gatherings are beginning to take a serious interest in portraying a more legitimate view of Anabaptism than the views of certain historians who can never get past the Münsterite uprising. This new interest in the Anabaptist movement can be attributed to the work of Mennonite scholars. While, as a black, I consider myself to be in strange territory when it comes to analyzing Anabaptist theology, I have found in it a dynamic challenge for theological inquiry.

I speak here as an amateur who happens to be concerned about socio-theological developments in the sixteenth century and its relation, if any, to socio-theological developments among Mennonites, especially this black Mennonite in the twentieth century. Keep in mind throughout this discussion that I speak to you from a black perspective, my own; not as an administrator, not as a Mennonite minister, not as a university student, even though I am at times one of the above. However, all the time I am black. When you fail to appreciate this fact about me you have committed a serious cultural mistake.

I will develop this chapter along four lines, discussing: (1) the historical character of Anabaptism; (2) the theological perspectives of the Anabaptists; (3) the paradox of blackness in viewing a Swiss story; and (4) the areas of Anabaptist theology that I as a black affirm.

The story of the Anabaptists grows out of the ferment of the sixteenth-century Reformation period. William R. Estep, in his book, *The Anabaptist Story,* defines the sixteenth century as an age of darkness. He writes,

> The sixteenth century was dark because it was the product of previous centuries. Civilization had become increasingly oblivious to human suffering and the value of the individual. Piety was evaluated by the amount of accumulated external acts. Hyprocrisy became the hallmark of the age. In the darkness the Anabaptists shone like so many meteors against the night.[2]

Anabaptism was a religious movement which emerged alongside of the religious and social discontent of that era in history. The Anabaptist wing of the Reformation originated in Zurich, Switzerland, in 1525. Prior to this date, the movement was stimulated and led by Ulrich Zwingli, a Swiss reformer and scholar. However, the early Anabaptists disagreed with Zwingli over the issue of a free church versus a state church. The result was a parting of company between him and the more radical brethren led by Conrad Grebel and Felix Manz. The Anabaptist movement suffered extreme persecution. The movement spread rapidly to practically every corner of Europe. Anabaptist fellowship groups emerged in places such as south Germany, Austria, and in the Netherlands. Ultimately large numbers of people joined the movement. H. S. Bender quotes Sebastian Franck, an opponent of the Anabaptists, as saying,

> The Anabaptists . . . soon gained a large following, . . . drawing many sincere souls who had a zeal for God, for they

> taught nothing but love, faith, and the cross. They showed themselves humble, patient under much suffering; they brake bread with one another as an evidence of unity and love. They helped each other faithfully, and called each other brothers. . . . They died as martyrs, patiently and humbly enduring all persecution.[3]

The movement had many groups and subgroups. There were many bodies in Anabaptism yet they were never really unified. Basically, this fact can be attributed to the Anabaptist view of church leadership and automony as well as the severe persecution that resulted. Another factor had to do with its newness. Differences of language, geography, and interpretation of the issues were evident. But in spite of these differences there were many points of similarity. We will examine some of these later.

Among the leaders of the movement were Conrad Grebel; Felix Manz, a humanist scholar; and Georg Blaurock, a former monk. These men and their associates constitute what is commonly called the "Swiss Brethren." These Swiss brothers were young men, gifted and full of vision. Other important figures included Balthasar Hubmaier, able leader and scholar; Hans Denck; Hans Hut, who was one of the most zealous and successful preachers among all Anabaptists; and Michael Sattler. One dare not overlook the influence of a Lutheran preacher named Melchior Hoffmann of north Germany, nor other leaders such as the Dutch brethren who produced Menno Simons, the former priest for whom the Mennonites are named.

Menno Simons is probably the most important figure in Anabaptism primarily because of his work in the consolidation of nonviolent Anabaptism particularly after the dreadful saga in Münster. Menno organized many congregations and laid down a foundation for our theological understanding of Christian faith. A contemporary of Menno was Pilgram Marpeck whose activity took place primarily in southern Germany and Switzerland. Others of the Dutch camp include Dirk and Obbe Phillips.

Art Gish, in his book, *The New Left and Christian Radicalism*, suggests that,

> As one reads sixteenth-century history, one is impressed with the parallels to our own century. There were the liberals who decided to work through the system and thus moderated their views so as not to offend the town council (Zwingli). There were the fiery revolutionaries (Müntzer) who preached violent overthrow of the system and the establishment of a just order composed of the disinherited. There were the conservatives (Luther) who defended the status quo and advocated brutal suppression of the peasants who refused to further oppression.[4]

I would add and there were the radicals who were the Anabaptists, a group comprised primarily of the alienated lower classes who were determined to follow Christ in all things. Franklin Littell has written,

> In contrast to many groups in history and in contemporary Christianity the Anabaptists actually meant what they said. The separation between verbalization and action which has been so marked in contemporary church groups can mislead us in our approach to the Anabaptist movement: the Anabaptists meant just what they said, and their teaching is unimportant apart from the direct attempt to give it embodiment in actual groups living in history.[5]

To view the Anabaptist movement in light of the sixteenth century is to consider that it was groups of people largely drawn from the oppressed determined to follow Christ. While the leadership that emerged was from a class of intellectuals and scholars, learned humanists and former priests, nonetheless the Anabaptists were mostly poor folks. Preserved Smith wrote of the Anabaptists:

> The most important thing about the extremists was not their habit of denying the validity of infant baptism and of rebaptizing their converts, from which they derived their name. What really determined their viewpoint and program was that they represented the poor, uneducated, disinherited classes. The party of extreme measures is always chiefly constituted from the proletariat because it is the very poor who most pressingly feel the need for change and because they have not usually the education to judge the feasibility of the plans, many of them quack nostrums, presented as panaceas for all their woes. A complete break with the past and with the existing order has no terrors for them, but only promise.

> A radical party almost always includes men of a wide variety of opinions. So the sixteenth century classed together as Anabaptists men with not only divergent but with diametrically opposite views on the most vital questions. Their only common bond was that they all alike rejected the authoritative, traditional, and aristocratic organization of both of the larger churches and the pretensions of civil society.[6]

H. Richard Niebuhr quotes Ernst Troeltsch who once wrote,

> The really creative, church-forming, religious movements are the work of the lower strata. Here only can one find that

union of unimpaired imagination, simplicity in emotional life, unreflective character of thought, spontaneity of energy and vehement force of need, out of which an unconditioned faith in a divine revelation, the naivete of complete surrender and the intransigence of certitude can rise.... All great community-building revelations have come forth again and again out of such circles and the significance and power for further development in such religious movements have always been dependent upon the force of the original impetus given in such naive revelations as well as on the energy of the conviction which made this impetus absolute and divine.[7]

Neibuhr states,

The religion of the untutored and economically disfranchised classes has distinct ethical and psychological characteristics, corresponding to the needs of these groups. Emotional fervor is one common mark. . . .

From the first century onward, apocalypticism has always been most at home among the disinherited. The same combination of need and social experience brings forth in these classes a deeper appreciation of the radical character of the ethics of the gospel and greater resistance to the tendency to compromise with the morality of power than is found among their more fortunate brethren. Again, the religion of the poor is characterized by the exaltation of the typical virtues of the class and by the apprehension under the influence of the gospel of the moral values resident in its necessities. Hence one finds here, more than elsewhere, appreciation of the religious worth of solidarity and equality, of sympathy and mutual aid, of rigorous honesty in matters of debt, and the religious evaluation of simplicity in dress and manner, of the wisdom hidden to the wise and prudent and meekness. Simple and direct in its apprehension of the faith, the religion of the poor shuns the relativizations of ethical and intellectual sophistication and by its fruits in conduct often demonstrates its moral and religious superiority.[8]

The Anabaptist movement during the Reformation is clearly a movement of oppressed peoples. It represented the political and economic as well as religious interest of the poor in proclaiming a faith which promised liberation and the establishment of a new Christlike Christian community.

Having discussed the Anabaptist movement in the setting of the Reformation period, let us analyze some of the major features of Anabaptist theology. The Anabaptists produced no great works of systematic theology. There are several reasons for this: (1) the Anabaptists were busy making disciple communities; (2) the Anabaptists, hunted and persecuted, did not have the time to pen theologies; and (3) the Anabaptists had a negative view of the state church theologian who simply justified the status quo. As J. C. Wenger of the Associated Mennonite Biblical Seminaries observes,

> The Anabaptists also feared that theology as such would lead in the direction of making God's Word ethically and spiritually irrelevant, whereas they wished to follow the Scriptures at any cost, believing that "No one can truly know Christ, except he follow Him in life" (Hans Denck) and that meant believing in the Christ presented in the Gospel, and obeying His Word in the power of the Holy Spirit.[9]

The Anabaptists tried to recover the first-century vision of the church, the true church. They patterned their life and style after first century Christians. H. S. Bender quotes Johann Loserth as saying:

More radically than any other party for church reformation the Anabaptists strove to follow the footsteps of the church of the first century and to renew unadulterated original Christianity.[10]

H. S. Bender, Mennonite theologian and scholar, suggests that the Anabaptist theology or vision included three main points of emphasis: (1) discipleship; (2) brotherhood; and (3) love and nonresistance. While this is true, a point of departure in my analyzing Anabaptist theology begins with two factors: (1) the concept of a believers' church and (2) the view of Scriptures.

The genius of the Anabaptist legacy is their concept of a believers' church. The church consists of those who have responded to Christ in a wide-awake, mature manner, those who have been claimed by Christ, those who have entered into a relationship with Him. Without that relationship there can be no church. Following Christ, walking in newness of life is for grown-ups, not babies. By grown-ups we mean those who respond because they understand what the gospel says and decide voluntarily to covenant with God and with His people. The believers' church is Christ's church, and because it is Christ's church it can never be an ethnic fellowship, a private club of restricted membership. The Anabaptists believed that membership in the believers' church is voluntary, and it is for all who would believe and be baptized. The Anabaptists did not believe that the church belonged to its members; rather the church belonged to Christ. The Anabaptists emphasized voluntarism and with this came the establishment of fellowships distinct from the established church and the other reformers of that day.

In matters such as the rejection of oaths, war, and infant baptism, the Anabaptists clearly stood apart from the civil religious concepts of that century. For tied to the principle of a voluntary believers' church was the Anabaptist concept of separation from the world and from the impingements of government. The Anabaptist concept of a believers' church included complete conformity to Christ and complete nonconformity to the world. Menno Simons, the noted Dutch preacher and unsung Anabaptist theologian, once declared,

> I for myself confess that I would rather die than to believe and teach my brethren a single word concerning the Father, Son, and Holy Ghost, at variance with the express testimony of God's Word, as it is so clearly given through the mouth of the prophets, evangelists, and apostles. [11]

On another occasion Menno said,

> You say we are inexpert, unlearned, and know not the scriptures. I reply: the Word is plain and needs no interpretation; namely, thou shalt love the Lord thy God with all thy heart, and with all thy soul, and with all thy strength, and thy neighbor as thyself. Matthew 22. Again, you shall give bread to the hungry and entertain the needy. Isaiah 58. If you live according to the flesh you shall die, for to be carnally minded is death. . . . [12]

The Anabaptist movement was characterized by total dependency upon God's Word, relying upon the Bible as a basis for theological life and thought. The living Word of God was alive for the Anabaptists. The Anabaptists insisted that it was important not only to hear the Word of the living God, but to obey the living God in all things. Menno Simons wrote on one occasion,

> The entire evangelical Scriptures teach us that the church of Christ was and is, in doctrine, life, and worship, a people separated from the world.[13]

The concept of nonconformity on the part of a people listening to God was a direct result of reliance upon the Word of God and a steadfast acceptance of the will of God.

Anabaptism to me represents the most constructive model of a believers' church response to a loving God. How then am I as a black Mennonite to relate to this Anabaptist past? What are the implications of sixteenth-century Anabaptism for minorities? What can we learn?

As a black Mennonite I am caught in a seemingly irreconcilable paradox. I am part of a conspicuous racial minority in a white-dominated, generally ethnic church, and at the same time living in a hostile white racist American society. What does a white American church heritage have to say to me, a powerless black man whose existence is threatened by the insidious tenacles of white racism? I'm not sure if placed in that context—probably very little. The fact that I am black is my ultimate reality and condition. It is impossible for me to stop being black or to surrender my basic reality for another's experience. Blacks have had to learn this lesson painfully down through the years. I want to know about the experience of others, and I think that it is important for others to know about me and to try to understand my experience. To gain insight into each other's experience can result in a meaningful and invigorating dialogue and respect.

Like most blacks, both past and present, I was introduced to Christianity through the white man. The white man sought to make me reject my concerns for this world as well as my blackness, and embrace the next world and his whiteness. I joined the Mennonite Church having had a genuine turning away from my sins to new life in Jesus Christ. I voluntarily entered into a covenant relationship with Christ and with the Mennonite Church, having been the recipient of good will and benevolence on the part of the Mennonites. In my years with Mennonites I have experienced a warm benevolence on the one hand, but a strange, cold austerity on the other hand. When I joined the Mennonite Church, I had no way of knowing what the relationship would be like. I started out quite young; I knew little Mennonite history and Mennonite thought.

As I began to attend Mennonite institutions such as Christopher Dock Mennonite High School and Goshen College, I discovered that Mennonites are a rather historical bunch. And I gained insight into the church's history and its tradition through familiarity with names like Menno Simons and Christopher Dock. I became acquainted with practices those of us who were new to the Mennonite Church thought of as being somewhat strange. Among the ordinances they observed were the holy kiss and foot washing—neither of which we had seen practiced before—and the doctrine of nonconformity to the world and of course nonresistance. All of these teachings were drilled into every Christian who identified with the Mennonite community and my pilgrimage through the church has not been any different.

I can speak here of my spiritual journey for it has had its ups and downs, its twists and turns, and its difficulties. I've struggled hard against negative thoughts, legalistic teachings, and the painful hurts that come as a result of being created in God's image. I have experienced the anguish of church splits and church fights. I have worked, played, and gone to school with Mennonites of practically all types. I have mixed feelings about the entire history of Mennonites and what it means for me as a minority in the church. I've raised many questions and probably one of the most perplexing has been, How does a person reconcile the paradox of being black and Mennonite? Where can I find those who have worked through the serious business of what it means to be black in the United States and then have proceeded to work through what it means to be a black Mennonite, a part of the believers' church heritage?

Very seldom do I talk about this and openly articulate the deep feelings that I have on this subject. On the one hand, I feel that I have been blessed in being a Mennonite. On the other hand, so have the Mennonites been blessed by my presence even though they brought me in through the back door. At least I analyze things in that way. Peeping through the keyhole has given me some insight into the fact that I am dealing with a serious ethnic community which has within the last twenty years questioned its own identity and is experiencing a crisis in that area. And those persons who have made the march through history have done it in a powerful and significant way. J. H. Nickels commented,

> The Mennonites have exhibited in this generation a vigor in historical studies unequalled, in proportion to their size, by any other Christian tradition in America....It seems to have arisen in part from the international crisis of identity of the Mennonites and their need to identify a viable tradition.[14]

I, too, share that look to the past out of a need for some sense of identity. Yet I have experienced a feeling that Anabaptism has been made so biological and so ethnic that persons like myself hardly know whether or not we should inquire or if in fact the territory is open for us to occupy. In the United States of America blacks have faced many closed doors. Every time I hear the term "our" forefathers, or "our" Mennonite heritage I instinctively wonder if I'm included in the term "our." Therefore, I think it is appropriate for me to ask the question, Is it possible for me to be really black and still feel an identity with the Anabaptist Mennonite tradition?

In trying to answer this question, I have done extensive reading and reflecting. I have spoken to other persons, and listened to other persons speak to me. In the entire process, I have tried to be in touch with what the Spirit is saying. In line with this search, my wife and I had the fine opportunity of traveling in Europe in 1971. We were a part of a group of Canadian and American Mennonites who accompanied Jan Gleysteen and Arnold Cressman on a study trip called "TourMagination II." The purpose of the tour in Gleysteen's words was "to become acquainted with certain aspects of 'our' history; the places where it actually happened." Thus we traveled to many localities where the Anabaptist movement took shape and places where the movement spread.

In touring the last remains of Anabaptist civilization, I must admit I could not always identify with what I saw or where I was. I sensed and felt and could understand what James Baldwin meant when he wrote,

I was a kind of bastard of the West; when I followed my

past I did not find myself in Europe but in Africa. And this meant that in some subtle way, in a really profound way, I brought to Shakespeare, Bach, Rembrandt, to the Stones of Paris, to the Cathedral of Chartres, and to the Empire State Building a special attitude. These were not my creations, they did not contain my history. I might search them in vain forever for any reflection of myself.[15]

Baldwin's words epitomize the emotional and intellectual anguish that black people experience whenever they try to find their identity amid historical categories that are white and not black. So I found extreme difficulty in searching for my past in Zurich, Holland, Switzerland, Germany, and the like. It just wasn't there!

My only identification in Europe was perhaps a spiritual one. The radical behavior of the Anabaptists, like that of the first-century church, stands as a witness of how I think we ought to live today. As a participant in the believers' free church life, I affirm the Anabaptist spiritual heritage. I believe that it is in looking back to where it all was formed that a black Christian can find a sense of direction and identification.

Unfortunately, the Mennonite community today has lost much of the historical spiritual quality of the Anabaptists. Mennonites today have drifted from the Anabaptist model of life and from the Anabaptist Christ. In fact, present-day Mennonites have replaced the Anabaptist Christ with an American one whose attitude toward blacks is obnoxious and abrasive. Former black Mennonite, Vincent Harding, has written an article entitled "Black Power and American Christ." In it he sounds the alarm of what young blacks like myself were saying during the days of black consciousness:

These young people say to America: "We know your Christ and His attitude toward Africa. We remember how His missionaries warned against Africa's darkness and heathenism, against its savagery and naked jungle heart. We are tired of all of this. This Africa that you love and hate, but mostly fear—this is our homeland. We saw you exchange your Bibles for our land. We watched you teach hymns to get our diamonds, and you still control them . . . you can keep your Christ."[16]

Harding further writes,

The American Christ is a Christ of separation and selfishness and relentless competition for an empty hole. We want no part of Him.[17]

Sincerely I think that somewhere along the way from Anabaptism to Mennonitism something drastic has taken place. In my estimation it is our Mennonite incompatibility with the Anabaptist Christ. As a black Mennonite living in these times of painful oppression and exploitation, I have to wonder what kind of Christ we are serving. I want nothing to do with an American Christ, a blue-eyed white dude that affirms the values of a sick and fallen society. I don't trust the American Christ. I wonder how much of this church which I have become a part of stands for what I deeply hate in America. I wonder if we will ever break out of the encirclement of racism. Preston Williams, a noted black scholar, wrote,

The consequence of white racism is black distrust. Blacks simply cannot trust whites, their systems of truth or their institutions of society.[18]

I wonder if there can ever be in the North American Mennonite form of Christianity any resemblance to the sixteenth-century model of discipleship.

As a poor black Mennonite, I affirm the Anabaptist Christ. I can identify with an Anabaptist Christ. The Anabaptist Christ led the Anabaptists to refuse to become a part of the institutional church. The Anabaptists were unimpressed by the vast institution the status quo establishment had become. The Anabaptists were disturbed by the conditions of the church. They insisted that it was a perversion of what Christ had in mind; the church had fallen. Their concern was for the recovery of the life and virtue of the early church.

A call for the restoration of the church was a major theme of the Anabaptists in this teaching and their writings. For the Anabaptists the church was to be a company of disciples who, having responded to Christ in a wide-awake voluntary manner, now formed His counter-community. The church constituted a minority fellowship within a persecuting society, a community of protesters. I agree with C. J. Dyck when he writes, "The uniqueness of the Anabaptist movement lies in the fact that it is a protest against unfaithfulness in the face of the biblical record, of the reformers themselves."

The Anabaptists protested the transformation of religion into an instrument that serves the interest of the state. The joining of the discipling voluntary community meant a break with the prevailing norms and values, with the established assumptions of the present order. All the authorities, institutions, political powers, historical forces, and social policies that demanded an absolute kind of allegiance had become idolatries. They were intruding between God and His people and between the people and themselves. In the community of faith, Christ's disciples had been freed from the rule of these rebellious principalities and powers. They were able to exercise and demonstrate freedom in relation to them. The Anabaptists had a clear doctrine of the state; there was little doubt among most of them that one thinks in terms of two entities, church and the world, the discipling community and Babylon. They believed firmly in the separation of a discipling community from the state. No magistrate or judge could dictate to them what their conscience, based on the Holy Word, had accepted.

I affirm the Anabaptist Christ because I find the Anabaptist Christ leading His people to affirm the centrality of the Word of God and to experience God at the feeling level. The Anabaptists as that voluntary society of new believers were bound to each other. But more than that, they had had a live emotional experience, a radical change of life that pressed to the core of their physical as well as their emotional and mental personhood. C. J. Dyck quotes Menno Simons as saying of his experience,

> My heart trembled in my body. I prayed God with sighs and tears that he would give me, a troubled sinner, the gift of His grace and create a clean heart in me, that through the merits of the crimson blood of Christ He would graciously forgive my unclean walk and ease-seeking life, and bestow upon me wisdom, candor and courage. . . .

> Behold thus, my reader, the God of mercy, through His abounding grace which He bestowed upon me, a miserable sinner, has first touched my heart, given me a new mind, humbled me in his fear, taught me in part to know myself, turned me from the way of death and graciously called me

into the narrow path of life, into the communion of His saints. To Him be praise forevermore. . . .[19]

The presence of the Holy Spirit was a fact of life among the early Anabaptists. They experienced the Holy Spirit at the feeling level. The Holy Spirit brought new birth and enabled them to be a viable manifestation of what it meant to be alive in Jesus Christ. In black gospel songs one gets the same sense of this feeling level transformation motif. One song says, "Well, I've already been to water; well, I've already been baptized; well, I've already been converted, and I feel, I feel, I feel all right, all right. Hallelujah, since I've been born again. Hallelujah, born again." Menno Simons talked the same kind of language,

> The new birth consists, verily, not in water nor in words, but it is the heavenly, living and quickening power of God in our hearts which comes from God, and by which the preaching of the divine Word, if we accept it by faith, quickens, renews, pierces, and converts our hearts, so that we are changed and converted from unbelief into faith, from unrighteousness into righteousness, from evil unto good, from carnality into spirituality, from earthly into the heavenly, (and) from the wicked nature of Adam into the good nature of Jesus Christ.[20]

The main issue as it related to the Anabaptists was whether or not they did in fact have a believers' church, a born-again community in which the Holy Spirit could function. And not only that, but at the feeling level did they experience all that God was? Did they understand all that God had to give to them? They spoke much of how God moved them, breathed into them new life, and this new life was visible and the manifestation of Jesus' life.

H. S. Bender in his article, "The Anabaptist Vision," writes,

> The Anabaptists could not understand a Christianity which made regeneration, holiness, and love primarily a matter of intellect, of doctrinal belief, or of subjective "experience," rather than one of the transformation of life. They demanded an outward expression of the inner experience. Repentance must be "evidenced" by newness of behavior.[21]

Throughout the history of black folks in the United States numerous stories, songs, books on receiving the gospel and newness of life communicate on a practical feeling level. New life is felt. Not only are the intellectual and the mental powers transformed, but also the physical and the emotional areas of one's life are touched by the powerful work of the Holy Spirit. Many can testify how "God reached out to me in my weakness and purchased me, a miserable sinner, and gave me a new heart, a new walk, and a new talk." In black theology this feeling level of theology is confirmed over and over again. I can affirm the Anabaptist Christ that makes this happen. As Mack Gobel says,

> The essential and distinguishing characteristic of this [Anabaptist] church is its great emphasis on the actual personal conversion and regeneration of every Christian through the Holy Spirit. This seems to me to point to a theology of personal experience, a theology of feeling level gospel in contrast to the secularized versions of regeneration.[22]

I affirm the Anabaptist Christ because the Anabaptist

Christ led the Anabaptists to become a serious Christian community. They identified with God's promise to the Israelites in Exodus 19:5,6 that, "if you will obey my voice and keep my covenant, you shall be my own possession among all peoples ... and you shall be to me a kingdom of priests and a holy nation."

It seems to me that the Anabaptists were able to understand the full extent of what it means to be a community faithful to Christ, a community that lives in contrast to the old society. A community that is not the result of an idealistic dream, but a community God is calling together. A true church community, not invisible but a fully visible community that practices dynamic obedience to God and to the will of God. A community that understands that it is not alone, that Christians need each other and rely upon each other for witness and for social outlook.

The early Anabaptists practiced mutual aid. They considered mutual aid as necessary and natural for a committed spiritual fellowship meeting in cellars, fields, gardens, and forests. The Anabaptists gathered food, money, and clothes for those in need. Members were encouraged to be a caring group that would reach out and be generous with others. The Anabaptists' view of property and economics were tied closely to their rule in life. The practice of mutual aid was a natural part of true discipleship. But their concern also extended to those outside the fellowship. There was a denial of individualism and an affirmation of community.

The Anabaptists taught nothing but faith, love, the cross, and caring and sharing with the brother in need and the brother in deed. This was the essential quality of the Anabaptist—they cared for all. The Anabaptist Christ led the Anabaptists to follow Him radically in all things. Following Him in all things meant that they were to carry on a caring relationship, a caring that would reject the dominant values of the sixteenth century. The Anabaptists did not merely talk about what it means to live a Christian life; they lived one. The Anabaptist Christ led the Anabaptists to reject compromise and to live by a new set of values, a new set of economics. Love and genuine caring were the marks of this fellowship—not only for the neighbor but for the brother. The Anabaptists could not do violence—not by word, by deed, or by sword. They did not take up arms against the other. To do so was clearly in opposition to the teachings of the Anabaptist Christ. While there were strong beliefs against using the sword, not all Anabaptists were nonresistant.[23]

The Anabaptists attempted to build a genuine believers' church based on the apostolic pattern of the New Testament. They lived in the reality of a new economic ethic which enabled them to be upset with injustice and unfaithfulness. For example, Menno Simons wrote in 1552 about the Protestant clergy,

> Is it not sad and intolerable hypocrisy that these poor people boast of having the Word of God, of being the true, Christian church, never remembering that they have entirely lost their sign of Christianity? For although many of them have plenty of everything, go about in silk and velvet, gold and silver, and in all manner of pomp and splendor; ornament their houses with all manner of costly furniture; have their coffers filled, and live in luxury and splendor, yet they suffer many of their own poor, afflicted members

(notwithstanding their fellow believers have received one baptism and partaken of the same bread with them) to ask alms; and poor, hungry, suffering, old, lame, blind, and sick people to beg their bread at their doors.

. . . Shame on you for the easygoing gospel and barren breadbreaking, you who have in so many years been unable to effect enough with your gospel and sacraments so as to remove your needy and distressed members from the streets. . . .[24]

In a caring community, everyone was concerned about the needs of the others so that the hungry would be fed, so that the thirsty would be given drink, so that the naked would have clothes on their back. All of this was done in relation to following the rule of Christ.

The Anabaptist Christ I affirm is a Christ who affirms the dignity and worth of all human beings. He led the Anabaptists to see clearly that all persons are invited to acknowledge the truth and share in the believers' church reality. The Anabaptists did not separate mind from body. Blacks in the Anabaptist view of personhood would not be looked upon as supermasculine menials with nothing to contribute to the community of faith. The Anabaptists, because of their identification with the Anabaptist Christ, were able to conquer feelings of superiority and hierarchy and leadership positions. Rather, they believed that nobody in the community of faith was more important than anyone else, but that all were significant. The Anabaptists believed in a covenant community, a kingdom of priests. A theology emerged—the priesthood of all believers. Inherent in the idea of priesthood of believers is the concept of equality. Every believer has the gifts and responsibility to spread the gospel, to share the good news. Don Jacobs in his 1967 World Conference address declared,

> It might be helpful to remind ourselves that the first generation of Anabaptists were the evangelists of Northern Europe. They themselves experienced in a fresh and remarkable way the presence of the living Lord who dwelt among them because of repentant faith and not simply because they received baptism. This became such a burning reality in their hearts that they were compelled to get the word around. It cost many of them their lives, but they died as they lived, full of light and life.[25]

Menno Simons, writing about the whole missionary thrust, said,

> This is my only joy and heart's desire; to extend the kingdom of God, reveal the truth, reprove sin, teach righteousness, feed hungry souls with the Word of the Lord, lead the straying sheep into the right path, and gain many souls to the Lord through His Spirit, power, and grace. . . .

> Therefore, we preach, as much as is possible, both by day and by night, in houses and in fields, in forests and wastes, hither and yon, at home or abroad, in prisons and in dungeons, in water and in fire, on the scaffold and on the wheel, before lords and princes, through mouth and pen, with possessions and blood, with life and death. We have done this these many years, and we are not ashamed of the gospel of the glory of Christ.[26]

Being a priesthood of believers meant that missionary life was not something that the elite did or something those who sat in high places did, but it was something that all the people did. They all shared the gospel with the common people and those who would listen. It is difficult to overemphasize the missionary zeal that characterized these early Anabaptist founders. Because of persecution they were driven in and out of exile. Nonetheless, they went everywhere spreading the good news. Donald F. Durnbaugh notes that "the Anabaptist women were considered to be as dangerous in speaking the illicit faith as their menfolk."[27] The spread of the gospel was not just a man's job, but it was also women's work. It was the duty of every church member to make the Great Commission relevant to their experience despite the known executions and torture, despite the persecution and suffering. Anabaptists believed that the church was called upon to suffer, that a follower of Jesus Christ could expect to suffer for his beliefs.

I affirm the Anabaptist Christ because He led the Anabaptists to understand what suffering means, what it means to be hurt, to be in pain, to be tortured and brutalized, to be harassed and hounded. Anabaptists suffered a great deal. There are many stories of how the Anabaptists ministered to each other in their pain and even to those who persecuted them. They lived a life of love in the face of torture and widespread persecution.

When the Anabaptists performed mission work, they did it as a joyful community spreading the good word about Jesus Christ and how He quickens and regenerates a life that has been ravaged by sin. They emphasized the grace He bestows on believers and how He gives a new sense of being, a new sense of peoplehood, a sense of somebodiness. All too often today in our churches we have not spread that kind of gospel. Instead, we have spread a gospel that is culturally oriented, a gospel that keeps people away from us and aloof from us. If in fact Jesus is good news we ought to share it; it is our background. In a report Paul Kraybill made to the Mennonite Church General Board, he said,

> The Anabaptist vision has not always been well communicated by us as missionaries. It is unfortunate that all too often Mennonite churches only see their uniqueness in their abstinence from smoking and drinking. There are very few who really understand the Anabaptist view of Scriptures and of the church and even less who are capable of creative theological thought.

From Anabaptism to Mennonitism we seem to have lost a ministry and I'm not at all sure why. I sometimes wonder why Mennonites, with their strange and peculiar history of dynamic missionary activity, have such a small number of followers in the world today. Have we lost the command, the commission to preach the gospel to every living creature and to call persons to something bigger than an ethnic past? Perhaps we have lost that particular vision. There is a need today for Mennonites to drop our alliance with society and its culture, and to again become a missionary movement that tries to recover the first century mode of outreach. Despite systematic suffering that will come, we need to spread the faith and not simply keep it to ourselves.

I can affirm the Anabaptist past because the Anabaptists were willing to be led by the Anabaptist Christ to reject the institutional status quo church. They were led to protest the marriage of church and state, led to experience God at the feeling level, led to a new concept of the person that enabled them to see individuals and their worth and dignity, their potential in the Lord. They saw persons who would be clothed with the gospel and themselves could be a part of the God-movement.

I affirm the Anabaptist past, their ethical insights and the values they stood for. I affirm their struggle for liberation. While I affirm the Anabaptist past and all that the Anabaptist Christ led the Anabaptists to do, I also affirm the emergence of black consciousness and black theological thought. It was black power that led blacks out of the wilderness of despair to a sense of hope and identity, not Anabaptism. Yet I can appreciate and understand the special significance of Anabaptism to me. I view Anabaptism as a movement, a movement of poor folks, oppressed peoples seeking liberation and the ushering in of God's kingdom for His will to be done on earth as it is in heaven.

Black history and black theological thought have some of the same elements as Anabaptism. Blacks in the past as today represent a powerless oppressed people yearning for liberation and justice, concerned about the moral pollution of the nation, striving for revolutionary change by any means necessary. By any means necessary I mean any means the oppressed think or feel appropriate for liberation to come. In the past this has meant prayer, nonresistance, violent outbreaks, Christian love, and a whole host of things as seen in the Anabaptist movement, too.

The struggle goes on. And for me, to be a black Christian whose spiritual roots and identity go back further than slavery, is an exhilerating experience. To recognize that I belong to a 400-year church history and a 500-year black history of struggling for humanization and Christian community is a beautiful thing. Most Mennonites, black and white, can only identify with the first century and they unfortunately bypass powerful chapters in the story of God's ongoing counter-community movement.

It seems to me that Mennonites in general and black Mennonites in particular who are trying to be obedient to Christ can gain a great sense of identity from the record of Anabaptists, as well as the movements of other oppressed peoples. In discussing the ongoing God movement blacks have a right to identify with this history. Blacks will find that the Anabaptists were a struggling minority—oppressed people who sought to restore the church to what the early church had been. Black history in America illustrates what the Anabaptists were like. We were struggling for freedom and human dignity denied to us by the church and by the unsaved society. The experience of the black community in the past and present is that of being a struggling minority, suffering persecution and abuse, but understanding our central link to a God who loves us and made us in His own image. We know, too, that Christ came into the world to challenge the powers of evil and to bring about our deliverance. We have found Jesus to be credible and believable, but not all those who call Him Lord, Lord are credible.

I believe we poor folks, we black folks, the disinherited, the Pentecostals, the charismatics, the radical Christians—we are today's Anabaptists. Most present-day Mennonites do not fit these categories, and have drifted away from what it means to be Anabaptist, from what it means to be part of a movement, part of a prophetic, dynamic oppressed minority that listens to God and not society. Hence, today the Mennonites hardly can be called the heirs of Anabaptism. As noted Mennonite scholar, John Howard Yoder, writes,

> This assumption that we are the Anabaptists is thus a source of some particular difficulties which we must now try to deal with. . . . To think of this would mean admitting as we never had to under the leadership of Funk and Coffman that we are not simply falling short of the Anabaptist vision; we are in our fundamental structures incompatible with it.[28]

Mennonites have become acculturated, melted down, average John Q. Middle-class Americans with all of society's vices, materialism, and arrogant snobbery! H. Richard Niebuhr says,

> Whenever Christianity has become the religion of the fortunate and cultured and has grown philosophical, abstract, formal, and ethically harmless in the process the lower strata of society find themselves religiously expatriated by a faith which neither meets their psychological needs nor sets forth an appealing ethical ideal.[29]

Who will reclaim the religiously unsophisticated, the poor humble folks of the land? Mennonites cannot in their present trend. I think we will need a new movement, a coalition of God's people—the young, the poor, the black and nonwhite people, the oppressed, and those who identify and have solidarity with the oppressed. Who are better prepared to lead a movement than the oppressed? The oppressed suffer the effects of oppression more than anyone else, therefore they are better able to understand the necessity of liberation.

The oppressed have something to offer the dominant

church. Oppressed black Mennonites need not be ashamed of our presence in a white-dominated church. We need only to understand who we are both in history and now. Whether Mennonites like it or not, God's gift to the Mennonite Church in this twentieth century is non-white. The gift is black. By black I am meaning all of the oppressed. To understand oppression is to know what it means to be black, for in the world today black is synonymous with oppression. As Baldwin once said, "The world is white no longer, neither is the church."

There has been a great deal of borrowing in the Mennonite past. Present-day Mennonites seeking to recover the Anabaptist Vision will likely need to engage in a borrowing and synthesizing process. Blacks with the emergence of black theology represent a dynamic resemblance of the Anabaptist past. Mennonites seeking to find themselves ought to look to black theology and to those black theologians who penned new theological consciousness amidst an American revolution. I believe they represent the ongoing impact of the God-movement.

In American theological circles black theology has a double perspective. It brings to theological reflection the particular and peculiar experiences of black people, and because that experience has been shaped in the vortex of oppression and persecution, it fundamentally relates to the Anabaptist heritage. Anabaptist theology reflects the ethnic and social experiences that include themes such as conversion, faithfulness, and the relational quality of mutual aid and brotherhood. These are linked to the black experience of oppression. We have in common a history of suffering and a drive for liberation as God's elect.

Mennonites seeking to recover the Anabaptist Vision can learn from the black church which refused to accept a Christianity that does not relate the message of the gospel to the humanizing of the social, economic, and political structures of society.

Looking to the black church, Mennonites will gain insight into the way blacks experience God at the feeling level. The black church worship patterns include elements of openness, free style encounter with God, and celebration of life. Worship in the black church tradition is a creative experience, not a book slavishly followed or a ritual rehearsed. The quietness, the apparent serenity, the supposed orderliness of worship in white Mennonite churches often serve to cover up a spiritual hollowness and narrowness that perpetuate the status quo and undergird racism.

Mennonites seeking the Anabaptist Vision through the black church experience will discover the prophetic tradition that characterizes the priestly function of the church throughout history. This tradition brings into judgment not only the institutions of society, but the institutional church as well. Mennonites will discover that to be a black Christian is in effect to be an Anabaptist.

Mennonites seeking to recover the Anabaptist Vision will need to align themselves with a different agenda. John Howard Yoder's prophetic observation is correct. He states,

> The agenda of the grass roots church is often not the Anabaptist agenda of mission and social change and reconciliation but the acculturation agenda.[30]

He goes on to say that Mennonites have become

concerned with such questions as when do we get an organ, or what do we do about the prayer veiling, when do we get a seminary-trained preacher, and when can we erect a church building that doesn't look like a barn? Such an agenda reflects a transition from a persecuted voluntary suffering minority to a middle-class affluent mentality.

And somewhere along the line there is a sense of hypocrisy in trying to say that we are the Anabaptists when we are not. I do not want to engage in the negative aspects of the confusion between Mennonites and Anabaptists, labeling everything good as Anabaptist and everything that is bad as Mennonite. But contemporary Mennonite theological leanings reflect an orientation toward wanting to be accepted by the present North American culture, society, and civil religion. At the same time Mennonites no longer want to be identified as a minority whose sense in mission is to be God's counter-community in a broken world. The revitalization of our denomination can happen when we usher in an age of concrete identification with the Anabaptist Vision, and not only hear about that vision, but respond with a new freshness to what that vision means for us today.

Mennonites seeking to recover the Anabaptist Vision will need to begin listening to us blacks and other non-whites, letting us have our turn at speaking. We do not become fully a part of the Mennonite family until we can tell others who we are, for we have heard white Mennonites tell us who they are. We are truly vehicles of God's ingenuity and God's infusion of new life in this twentieth century. A dynamic movement can happen if all of us as Mennonites begin to synthesize the reality of being black in a racist world that is torn apart with a strong desire to recover the sixteenth-century Anabaptist Vision with all of its sociological implications and theological soundness. We need each other. Our mutual dependence requires mutual assistance at every phase of our Christian existence in a church we both voluntarily covenanted with for the glory of God.

4

CHRISTIAN FAITH IN BLACK AND WHITE

To be brothers and sisters in the Lord we must understand the dynamics of black/white relations and its implications in Christian faith. An examination of the historical nature and development of black/white relations is necessary for understanding the status and reality of that relation today.

Briefly, the historical relationship of blacks and whites is characterized by a master/slave mentality—which has made it impossible for the two races to communicate. The grounds for comunication—equality, mutual responsibility, and mutual trust—were destroyed. Whites have related to blacks primarily from a role of assumed superiority. Whites enter the circumference of the relationship feeling that everything of value is on their side, and that blacks have nothing to offer. Whites relate to blacks on a powerful/powerless basis. In recent years the relationship existing between the two groups has differed from the past in degree but not in kind. Whether the relationship be master/slave, boss/laborer, welfare worker/recipient, policeman/ghetto youth, board of church/black administrator, it is always beginning from the same base, a powerful/powerless and exploiter/victim relationship.

Blacks have responded to this type of white domination

with deep feelings of rage and rebellion. The injustice of the situation has been obscured by paternal and bene-volent acts by whites from time to time.

What is the cause of this unhealthy relationship? I believe it is racism. Racism as experienced in America is more than a sickness. It is a religion, a religion to which millions of people in one way or another give allegiance. Its theology says, "White is right." At first racism was basically confined to the area of economics. Later it ac-quired an ideological and finally a religious justification. Today, despite all the historic consequences and realities of the evils of slavery and nominal recognition of the wrongness of that system of oppression, the average person still fails to recognize a viable black presence in America. Racism makes it impossible for most whites to accept someone as both human and black. They say, "Why, Hubert, I don't see you as a black. I see you as a human being." In other words, my color offends them and they are shamed and embarrassed by it. They will ac-cept my humanity only to the extent that they can ignore my color.

Racism comes naturally and systematically to whites. It is generated by culture and reflected in and through all of its institutions and systems without exception. White racism is far from being the simple delusion of a bigoted and ignorant group of people. White racism is a set of beliefs whose structures arise out of the deepest levels of American life—from the fabrics of assumptions that are made about the world, about whites themselves, and fun-damentally about blacks and others. The dynamics of black/white relations are subsumed within the concepts of racism and discrimination. Discrimination is different from racism. The white pastor who hates blacks but does nothing to deprive blacks of their rights is racist but cannot be accused of discrimination. On the other hand, the white college that systematically and arbitrarily assigns blacks as roommates with blacks or advocates separate dormitories for black students because "they feel more comfortable with their own kind" is discriminating.

An unfortunate consequence of racism and discrimination is that whites fail to understand their own ethnic differences and commonalities. Racism and racial separatism continue to flourish in America today. White hostility toward blacks has reached an all-time high; blacks are reciprocating. The turmoil spills over into every institution affecting black/white relations in all settings. Harmonious black/white relations are difficult to achieve and maintain. Blacks and whites have moved further apart today, both physically and psychologically. As blacks continue to find themselves and their identity, whites remain unable to establish a base for comfortable relationships built on mutual trust and confidence.

The black and white worlds are separated and with each passing day drift further and further apart. The issue facing us is, How can we liberate ourselves from racism and racial polarization? Or perhaps a better question might be, How can we begin to develop authentic black/white relations? This question is a difficult one, and one of particular interest because it affects the development of God's people and the future of the believers' church.

The assumption that black/white relations can be transformed into a harmonious and authentic relationship finds its basis in the New Testament, as exemplified in the words of the Apostle Paul,

Therefore, if any one is in Christ, he is a new creation; the old has passed away, behold, the new has come. All this is from God, who through Christ reconciled us to himself and gave us the ministry of reconciliation . . . (2 Cor. 5:17, 18).

To be in Christ is to be Christian; to be Christian is to act in accordance with the Bible; to act in accordance to the Bible means reconciliation; reconciliation is the theological basis for facilitating authentic black/white relations. During certain periods in history we do have evidence that the church through some of its members characterized the "new creation" motif. When this occurred, healthy black/white relationships existed. I can think of times when authentic white Christians joined with blacks in actively opposing the evils of racism and discrimination in this oppressive society and gave full support to the rejection of a white-dominated frame of thinking and operation.

Authentic relations require give and take, sensitivity, mutual trust and respect, understanding and affirmation of each other's cultural differences, and moving to a positive state from a negative one on the love/hate continuum. We live in a pluralistic society. Black people and white people are locked together in such a way that each determines the other's fate. An authentic black/white relationship will emerge when the two groups, having distinct and conspicuous differences, fully accept and recognize these differences and relate to each other as equals. It will come when both of us communicate and appreciate the differences we have as a source of mutual enrichment and learning.

The goals and strategies of facilitating black/white

relationships must be approached in terms of the realities. First of all, in developing black/white relations, one must know that the integration model is dead. The integration model no longer provides an adequate approach to black/white relations. Integration as it has been practiced is totally rejected by blacks. The integration approach is too one-sided. It leaves black men the sole task of telling about their dreams concerning justice and equality for all. The integration approach as defined by whites means everything moves from black to white. It is unfortunate how integration was defined solely by whites for white purposes. Under their definition the black experience is completely wiped out. The white integration model failed because black folks could not determine their own destiny. Preston Williams writes,

> The rejection of integration as it has been practiced means simply that, no more, no less. It points to the desire on the part of the black man for a new shape and form for the relationship between black and white.

It did not take long before a large number of blacks saw what was happening through integration and cried out for "black power." Blacks taking their cues from Malcolm X, Stokley Carmichael, and other black awareness writers, poets, and artists began a drive away from the integration model into a separatism and black nationalism model.

It would appear to me that white Christians still hold fast to the dream of integration, while, on the other hand, blacks have extreme difficulty with the integration approach, opting for a strong separatism model. I'm not so

certain that separatism is a good model either. Vernon
Dixon, editor of the book, *Beyond Black or White*, writes,

> But black and white Americans who adopt the either/or
> approach cannot tolerate the existence of racial and cultural
> differences. Each sets up its own collective uniqueness as the
> universal culture, the common culture, the valid and valu-
> able culture. Each, therefore attempts to obliterate the
> other's cultural uniqueness to bring the actual black-white
> America into conformity with its conceptualized world of
> all-black or all-white. Each seeks to achieve *e pluribus
> unum*, its one out of many. . . .

> . . . the application of the either/or conceptual approach
> to race relations produces racial harmony when the blacks
> and whites embody total sameness. Because they are both
> the same and different, ordering black and white expe-
> riences in either/or terms necessarily causes racial polarity
> and conflict.[2]

Under an either/or model of Christian faith, I would
need to become a Black Muslim, for I would conceive of
the world as all black. An ethnic Mennonite would
conceive of the world as all white. It will be difficult to
bring about black/white harmony until these concep-
tualizations are changed. Seeing only one race or the
other as relevant leads to an either/or approach in black/
white relationships. In an either/or approach everything
falls into one category or the other but nothing can
belong to more than one category at the same time. In an
article entitled "The Diunital Approach to Black-White
Relations," Vernon Dixon helped me to see the difficulties that arise whenever people attempt to function from a
position of total exclusion or total inclusion. Dixon writes,

In race relations, black falls into the category of non-white, and white falls into the category of non-black, therefore, the either/or habit of mind easily allows one to conceive of black and white as mutually exclusive opposites. Then only black is relevant, or only white is relevant.[3]

In contrast to whites, blacks possess a twoness. Blacks are sealed in both blackness and whiteness. Whiteness is, and has always been, synonymous with American culture, a culture born in Europe. And white culture is radically different from black culture. Whites are tied to and locked into a culture that does not permit them to move beyond and understand other cultures. Margaret Walker, poet, and professor of English at Jackson State College, writes,

> The white American is basically ignorant of the cultures of other people, and has no appreciation for any other language, art, religion, history, or ethical system save his own. He is in no way prepared to live in a multiracial society without hostility, bigotry, and intolerance. He believes that he must convert all people to his way of thinking because he cannot possibly conceive that his way of thinking may not always be right for everyone else. Everyone must dress, think, pray, and amuse himself as he does.[4]

Whites are imprisoned in cultural racism, and the question that is left to be answered is whether or not whites can break out of their prison lifestyles, or whether in fact whites want to.

According to Dixon, blacks operate from a cultural framework that can be described as "diunital." Dixon constructed this neologism by taking Webster's definition of "di," and the word "unit," and adding the adjectival form, "al." The literal meaning of diunital is "something apart and united at the same time."[5] Dixon says,

> American blacks rather than whites are more deeply attuned to a diunital existence for two reasons. First, we live in a dual existence. We are American citizens, yet we are not. American institutions are ours, yet they are not. We have one identity that are two identities. This experience of living two lives in one results from the inability of American whites to accept blacks as blacks. Thus we tend toward thinking diunitally as a reaction to our exclusion by whites from the status of full-fledged Americans.[6]

As mentioned earlier, black people possess a twoness, a double consciousness, a strange feeling of duality. On the one hand they are united to the white society, but on the other hand they are separated and rejected by that society.

Whites are culturally deprived, lacking the experience of living and operating from two different cultures, lacking also authentic appreciation of cultures other than their own. Whites will need to acquire "soul," that is, this twoness, this feeling of living in two worlds, and adopt a diunital approach. Dixon's diunital approach states:

> Americans who adopt this approach start from the conceptual position that acknowledges blackness and whiteness as authentic, valid, and valuable. The conceptual world of black and white is identical to the actual world. No longer must they reconcile these two worlds by assimilating or destroying cultural differences. According to the diunital approach black and white desire to perpetuate the existence and development of both ethnic cultures. One way to achieve cultures is through what I call the theory of cultural diunity. The national culture, rather than being synonymous

with whiteness, now becomes a union of opposite or different cultures.[7]

Dixon recognizes the differing cultural norms of each group, based on racial grouping, and also that each group may maintain its own institutions or participate in the same institutions. To be culturally diunital means that individual institutions are exclusive and inclusive in nature. Dixon says,

> In this period of increasing social polarization and conflict I hope that the diunital approach may suggest to other people a way in which they too can be pro-black without being anti-white and be pro-white without being anti-black. This means an alternate America in which people mutually acknowledge the authenticity, validity, and value of black and white cultures.[8]

What are the implications for a diunital model in the Christian community of faith? As a black Christian within the Mennonite Church, a white-oriented structure, I see the validity of a diunital conceptual approach, I am committing myself to facilitating reconciliation and racial harmony. As Dixon writes,

> According to the diunital concept of ordering experiences, I resolve my identity crisis in this way: I simultaneously embody a black ethnic identity and a white American or national identity; I am both these different identities without inherent antagonism; I am at once black and not black. This is my blackness.[9]

Thus, as a Mennonite I embrace Anabaptism, and as a black, I embrace black theology, and I affirm both.

Rather than an integration model which is repulsive to blacks, and the either/or model which has implications for total exclusiveness and separatism, why not adopt the diunital model? A diunital approach will serve to strengthen black awareness and ethnocentrism rather than dilute it. In light of the fact that the Protestant church is one of the most segregated institutions in America, it appears to me that whites would benefit greatly from this model. It would mean the end to polarization and cultural racism which now alienates whites from blacks and other nonwhites. Further, it would introduce an alternative to the white man's evangelical bent toward white integration which in reality is suicidal for blacks and whites.

J. E. K. Aggrey of Nigeria says:

> You can play a tune of sorts using the white keys alone, and a tune of sorts using black keys alone. But for the best harmony, you must play both the black and white keys.[10]

The only viable solution for America and indeed, the church, is the diunital approach. It is on the church that the moral injunction to form a community of blacks and whites together falls most heavily. What would happen if we who are a part of the community of faith, and who long for the community of faith to be an effective tool for change, began to see the church as an object of change? Would this not affect our theology? How? What help could theology be, anyway? Theology is a person's critical reflection on the Christian community in light of God's activity as recorded in the Bible. Gustava Gutierrez in his book, *A Theology of Liberation*, writes,

The Christian community professes a faith which works through charity. It is—at least ought to be—real charity, action and commitment to the service of men. Theology is reflection, a critical attitude.[11]

There is need for a diunital approach to theology. In constructing a diunital approach to Christianity or a theology of liberation we begin with the following set of assumptions:

1. *The first assumption is that black theology's critique of white American Christianity is valid and significant.* It is the truth. It is the truth on two levels—sociologically and biblically. Sociologically, it is undeniably true that institutional Christianity in America still is infested with perverse racism. Further, institutional Christianity in America has allowed itself to become the defender of the status quo and is thereby running counter to the work of God.

Biblically, it is undeniably true that the gospel is the good news of God in Christ encountering humans in the depth of their oppression, liberating them from all human and satanic forces which hold them captive. When Jesus preached His first sermon He alluded to His mission and ministry. (See Luke 4:18,19.) This was not only true of the ministry of Jesus, but characterized the actions of God throughout history. The God of Israel was known by what He was doing in history for the salvation-liberation of His people. Jesus was simply the Holy Child of God doing His Father's business.

In keeping with a diunital approach to theology, I affirm the sixteenth-century radical critique of the church and draw from the Anabaptists the concept of restoration of the church. I see this as being more valid than the idea of renewal.

2. *The second assumption is that a diunital approach to a theology of liberation affirms the liberation theme as being valid, useful, and the gospel.* We do not regard liberation theologies as a contemporary fad, or "the dominant vogue of with-it theology." To us, the biblical story in both the Old Testament and the New Testament is the story of God's liberating activity. As white Christian Joseph Barndt wrote in his book, *Liberating Our White Ghetto:*

> The Christian gospel has not changed. It is the same today as it always has been. It is a gospel of liberation for an oppressed people. It is good news to the poverty stricken in the ghettos of our land. It is the proclamation of liberty to the captives in our prisons and on our reservations. It is sight to the blind, strength for the lame, community for the lonely. It is freedom for oppressed people of America and the world.... This does not mean, however, that liberation is only for the poor, black and powerless, and not for white middle-class suburbanites. White middle-class suburbanites need to be liberated as much as anyone else.[12]

Barndt further writes in speaking as white to white:

> You and I must consider ourselves oppressed people. Not only are we enslaved to false values, greed, callousness, exploitive powers, and corruption, but we are being oppressed and harassed by many of the same dehumanizing forces of our society that beset those who are not white and middle class.... As white middle-class Americans, we can understand freedom only insofar as we identify ourselves with the oppressed. And one of the indicators of our oppression is our racism.[13]

As cultural diunital Christians we seek to borrow from sources other than the Puritan mainstream of theological thought. Our theology springs from many differing cultural molds. Therefore, in articulating a theology of liberation we accept the radical theology of our Latin American brothers and also the theology of contemporary black theologians, understanding that critical evaluation and analysis will take place and we will seek to keep God's Word written central and pivotal.[14] To use God's Word as the center of liberation theology and all discourses on the work of God is to reflect the Anabaptist stream of history and the believers' church tradition. We affirm them as being valid for our contemporary probing of the Christian faith.

3. *A third assumption is that Jesus Christ is Lord and Liberator.* C. S. Lewis was correct when he said, "Either this man was and is the Son of God or else a madman or something worse. You can shut Him up for a fool, or you can spit at Him and kill Him as a demon or you can fall at His feet and call Him Lord and God." We contend that Jesus is Lord, and we are committed to a radical following of Him. A diunital view will draw heavily from an Anabaptist view of what it means to follow Jesus. Contemporary America has, as Vincent Harding writes, "Americanized" Jesus so that He reflects white middle-class norms. To follow that kind of Jesus will lead to destruction. We recognize that Christian theology begins and ends with Jesus Christ. There can be no Christian theology without Jesus Christ being the center, the main ingredient. The diunital approach to Christ sees Him as one who set forth the example of diunital living.

To understand the historical Jesus without seeing His

identification with cultures other than His own is to distort His person and twist the truth. Jesus was an oppressed minority, a poor man seeking to do the will of His Father God who sent Him. A diunital approach sees the image of Christ as suited to, and in the context of, individual tribes and cultures. Therefore we insist that theologically there be a black Messiah, an African Christ, an Indian Christ, A Chicano Christ, a white Christ. Each racial entity will reflect Christ in their own image. We believe this is good, for it precludes an either/or approach. The opening words of Black Christian Nationalist leader Albert Cleage, Jr.'s book, *The Black Messiah*, deals with how whites for years tried to force its blue-eyed, blond-haired Jesus on the world. Cleage writes:

> For nearly 500 years the illusion that Jesus was white dominated the world only because white Europeans dominated the world. Now, with the emergence of the nationalist movements of the world's colored majority, the historic truth is finally beginning to emerge—that Jesus was really a non-white leader of a non-white people struggling for national liberation against the rule of a white nation, Rome.[15]

Cleage further talks about whites who still insist on giving credence to the racist assumption of whites that everything good and valuable has to be white. From a personal perspective my Christ is not now, nor can He ever be, a white Christ. If He is, then the Bible is a lie, and I am not made in His image, black and beautiful. My Christ is the black Messiah. He knows my history. He understands my culture. He speaks my language. I come to Him and cry out, "My Lord and my God." Yet, I believe Christ will need to be Christ for all peoples of all colors. I resist insisting on a black Christ to the exclusion of other colorful Christs. There is a real danger of an either/or approach to Christology and the shape and image of Christ among oppressed peoples. While one could dwell on the coloration of Christ, it is of serious importance that one does not overlook the essence of Christology which has to do with the proclamation of good news centered in the cross and resurrection of Jesus Christ. The cross is primary. We must encounter the cross, not from a secondhanded experience, but firsthandedly, understanding that,

> He was wounded for our transgressions, he was bruised for our iniquities; upon him was the chastisement that made us whole, and with his stripes we are healed (Isaiah 53:5).

The resurrection is the sequel to the cross experience. The resurrection is central to the New Testament faith. It was central for the early church. They lived and gave witness to the fact that "God has made him both Lord and Christ, this Jesus whom you crucified." The resurrection indicates the power of God in Christ over death. A diunital approach to witnessing is one of proclaiming everywhere I go, as best I know how, that "I serve a risen Saviour, He's in the world today/I know that He is living ... He lives, He lives ... you ask me how I know He lives— He lives within my heart." He is present now, wanting to make us "fishers of men," wanting us to take up our cross and follow Him, no turning back, no turning back.

4. *A fourth assumption is that a diunital theology of liberation sees the Christian faith as having radical im-*

plications on human life and society, and as presenting a convincing paradigm for revolutionary social change. The Christian faith as introduced by Jesus and continued by the early disciples is satisfying, not only spiritually, but intellectually, ethically, and emotionally. The Christian faith supplies a set of ethical values for measuring problems and constructing solutions. The foundation for all of this is firmly grounded in the life of Jesus Christ. Jesus gives an absolute standard of measurement. It is therefore possible to detect the wrongness of discrimination, pollution, and the awfulness of war and human conflict.

The way to change is in dipping into the life-giving water of the life-giver Jesus. The changed person is the new person. 2 Cor. 5:17. Unless a change occurs, we will continue to deal with effects and not causes. As new persons of God we are called to be stewards of all that God has made. We are called to take care of the world. Genesis 1:28. Unlike secular revolutionists, we are to uphold the dignity and worth of all peoples, working for the new order of Jesus Christ and the coming of His kingdom. We live in the reality that it is already taking shape. We pray, "Thy kingdom come; keep coming." We bear witness to God's plan for this earth both orally and actively. Matthew 5:16. We are to act as a people, not as individuals. We are to be a people born anew, a revolutionary third force, radical disciples, bearing witness without compromise or paralysis, impelled by God's Spirit, salting and lighting the earth.

5. *A fifth assumption is that diunital theology will create a counter-community of faith, a dedicated minority disciplined by God.* He is calling us to be an authentic voice crying in the wilderness of Western sick

society. The diunital approach to Christian community means that the culturally diunital Christian is a part of God's new people, a counter-community called into being by God through Jesus Christ. This Christian counter-community represents God's new thing. Isaiah 43:19; Revelation 21:5. The call of God in Jesus creates this counter-community, not just people deciding they want to be together. That call is to be with Jesus and in Jesus and to go out and be fruitful and multiply, creating the need for more counter-communities to spring up in America and throughout the world. Mark 3:14. God's counter-community is always represented by people of different cultural backgrounds. Galatians 3:27, 28. James Cone rightly says,

> . . .the church by definition, contains no trace of racism. Christ "has broken down the dividing walls of hostility" (Eph. 2:14)[16]

> The church is not bound by standards of race, class, or occupation. It is not a building or an institution. It is not determined by bishops, priests, or ministers as these terms are used in their contemporary sense. Rather, the church is God's suffering people.[17]

Jesus' call is also to heal those who are sick. Art Gish in his book, *The New Left and Christian Radicalism*, writes, "We are called to make a sick world well." God's intention today is for healthy communities of faith to counter the sickness that permeates North American life. Racism, militarism, and sexism are the basic sicknesses in America, and the salt and light of a counter-community of faith are desperately needed. God's counter-community is known by the love ethic shown for one another. That love ethic is drawn from New Testament models and from the example of the Anabaptists.

6. *A final assumption is that a diunital theology will have in it a sense of celebration drawn from the emerging theologies of liberation.* In proposing a diunital approach to a theology of liberation I am suggesting that a black Christian in the Mennonite Church can be pro-black without being anti-white, and white Mennonites can be pro-white without being anti-black. This means that I can relate with the traditions and histories of white forefathers, while at the same time being a part of the black past and the present black struggle for liberation. I see a need for Christian people, both white and nonwhite to mutually accept and affirm the authenticity, validity, and value of each other's cultures.

A diunital approach to theology suggests to me the concept of transcending. The phrase, "We shall overcome," is a thematic expression that has emerged in recent history and is linked with the late civil rights activist, Dr. Martin Luther King, Jr. When "we shall overcome" was utilized by King it implied more than to master, suppress, surmount, or prevail over an obstacle. The term "transcend" more accurately describes King's meaning of overcome. Transcend means "to go beyond the limits of" and I would add "to go beyond the limits of one's own cultural ethos into another. To be a part of your culture and another's at the same time. To be a part of your theological past and another at the same time." A diunital approach utilized by Christians is the achievement of overcoming or transcending. In religious circles this concept will need to be given more attention, particularly in articulating a theology of liberation.

The church ought to be an institution within which authentic black/white relationships and theologies emerge, making it possible for the church to function as the leaven that will make human life more human. To be human and to act in a way that makes life more human in the racist world should be our constant goal. Faith sees the possibility of a new fellowship formed from union of opposites. To be Christian is to act as a facilitator in creating the union of blacks and whites, committed Christians with a diunital conceptual framework and a Christian theology of liberation. For both blacks and whites a diunital approach will use the good from both the white and black religious and cultural experience as a basis for contemporary American theology.

NOTES

Chapter 1: On Being Black in a White Church

1. William F. Cross, Jr., "Discovering the Black Referent: The Psychology of Black Liberation," In Vernon J. Dixon and Badi Foster, *Beyond Black or White: An Alternate America* (Boston: Little, Brown and Co., 1971), p. 100.

2. *Ibid*, p. 101.

3. Preston N. Williams, "Ethics and Ethos of the Black Experience," *Christianity and Crisis*, May 1971, pp. 104-109.

4. James Baldwin, *The Fire Next Time* (New York: Dell, 1962), p. 130.

5. James Juhnke, "Mennonite Benevolence and Civic Identity," *Mennonite Life*, January, 1970.

6. Albert Cleage, Jr., in "The Black Messiah and the Black Revolution," *Quest for a Black Theology*, edited by James J. Gardiner and J. Deotis Roberts, (Philadelphia: Pilgrim Press, 1971), pp. 6, 7.

7. Irvin B. Horst, "Mennonites and the Race Question," a paper.

8. Merle Good, *Hazel's People* (Herald Press, 1975) was made into a motion picture starring Geraldine Page and Pat Hingle. The story portrays a non-Mennonite youth's first encounter in a Mennonite community located in southeastern Pennsylvania.

9. Lawrence J. Burkholder, "The New Mennonite Community," *Forum*, February 1973, pp. 2,3.

Chapter 2: An Analysis of Black Theology

1. Robert McAfee Brown, *The Spirit of Protestantism* (New York: Oxford University Press, 1965), page 118.

2. James H. Cone, in the introduction to his book, *Black Theology and Black Power* (New York: Seabury Press, 1969), mentions that his book was written with "a certain dark joy." I experienced the same pain and joy.

3. Joseph A. Johnson, *The Soul of the Black Preacher* (Philadelphia:

United Church Press, 1971), p. 87. Copyright © 1971 United Church Press, used by permission.

4. *Ibid.*, p. 87.

5. James H. Cone, "Black Consciousness and the Black Church," *Christianity and Crisis*, Vol. XXX, November 2, p. 249.

6. R. Rodgers Cornish, "A New Theology for a New People," *The Christian Century*, September 16, 1970, p. 1080.

7. J. Deotis Roberts, *Liberation and Reconciliation: A Black Theology* (Philadelphia: Westminster Press, 1971), p. 18.

8. Joseph R. Washington, Jr., *Black and White Power Subreption*, Boston: Beacon Press, 1971), p. 18.

9. Cone, *Black Theology and Black Power, op. cit.*, p. 130.

10. Major J. Jones, *Black Awareness: A Theology of Hope* (New York: Abingdon, 1971), p. 14.

11. Cone, *op. cit.*, p. 43.

12. Jones, *op. cit.*, p. 12.

13. *Ibid.*, p. 13.

14. Russell L. Adams, *Great Negroes: Past and Present*, ed. D. P. Ross, Jr. (Chicago: Afro-Am Publishing Co., 1964), p. 7.

15. James H. Cone, *A Black Theology of Liberation* (Philadelphia: Lippincott, 1970), p. 31.

16. Johnson, *op. cit.*, p. 88.

17. Jones, *op. cit.*, p. 15.

18. Johnson, *op. cit.*, p. 155.

19. *Ibid.*, p. 154.

20. *Ibid.*, p. 154.

21. Carleton L. Lee, "Toward a Sociology of the Black Religious Experience," *The Journal of Religious Thought*, Summer 1973, p. 12.

22. *Ibid.*, p. 12.

23. John Powell, "Toward a Unified Theology," an unpublished paper.

24. Quoted in Benjamin E. Mays', *The Negro's God as Reflected in His Literature* (New York: Atheneum, 1969), p. 132.

25. Mays, *Ibid.*, p. 133.

26. Roberts, *op. cit.*

27. Mays, *op. cit.*, p. 168.

28. Quoted in Mays, *Ibid.*, p. 168.

29. J. E. Lowery, "Behold a Black Horse: A Presentation of Black Theology."

30. Roberts, *op. cit.*, p. 176.

31. Washington, *op. cit.*, p. 139.

32. Baldwin, *op. cit.*, p. 21.

Chapter 3: An Analysis of Anabaptism

1. Walter Klaassen, *Anabaptism: Neither Catholic nor Protestant* (Waterloo, Ont.: Conrad Press, 1973), p. 1.
2 William R. Estep, *The Anabaptist Story* (Grand Rapids: Eerdmans, 1975), p. 20.
3. Harold S. Bender in "The Anabaptist Vision," *The Recovery of the Anabaptist Vision*, edited by Guy F. Hershberger (Scottdale, Pa.: Herald Press, 1957) p. 46.
4. Art Gish, *The New Left and Christian Radicalism* (Grand Rapids: Eerdmans, 1970), p. 52.
5. *Ibid*, p. 59, quoting Littel.
6. Preserved Smith, *Reformation in Europe* (New York: Collier Books, 1962), p. 84.
7. H. Richard Niebuhr, *The Social Sources of Denominationalism* (Gloucester, Mass.: Peter Smith), p. 29.
8. *Ibid.*, pp. 30, 31.
9. J. C. Wenger, *The Mennonite Church in America* (Scottdale, Pa., 1966), p. 255.
10. Bender, *op. cit.*, pp. 37, 38.
11. Wenger, *op. cit.*, p. 260.
12. Wenger, *op. cit.* p. 260
13. Guy F. Hershberger, editor, *The Recovery of the Anabaptist Vision* (Scottdale, Pa.: Herald Press, 1957), p. 48.
14. Footnoted in the epilogue of Donald F. Durnbaugh's book, *The Believer's Church* (New York: Macmillan, 1970), p. 301.
15. James Baldwin, *Notes of a Native Son* (New York: Bantam Books, 1968), p. 4.
16. Vincent Harding in "Black Power and the American Christ," *The Black Power Revolt*, edited by Floyd B. Barbour (Boston: Porter Sargent, 1969), pp. 87, 88.
17. *Ibid.*, p. 89.
18. Preston N. Williams, "Ethics and Ethos of the Black Experience, *Christianity and Crisis*, May 1971.
19. C. J. Dyck, " The Life of the Spirit in Anabaptism," *Mennonite Quarterly Review*, Vol. XLVII, October 1973, pp. 318, 319.
20. J. C. Wenger, editor, *The Complete Works of Menno Simons* (Scottdale, Pa.: Herald Press, 1956). p. 215.
21. Bender, *op. cit.*, p. 43.
22. Quoted in Dyck, *op. cit.*, p. 312.
23. For a better understanding of the point I'm making, one should read James Stayer's *Anabaptist and the Sword* (Lawrence, Kan.: Coro-

nado Press, 1972), and see H. S. Bender's footnotes in his Anabaptist Vision article in Hershberger's *The Recovery of Anabaptist Vision, op. cit.*

24. Quoted by Klaassen, *op. cit.*, p. 60.

25. Donald R. Jacobs, "The Witness of the Holy Spirit in Evangelism," *Proceedings of the Eighth Mennonite World Conference*, C. J. Dyck, ed., p. 46.

26. Wenger, *op. cit.*, p. 75.

27. Durnbaugh, *op. cit.* p. 232.

28. John Howard Yoder, "Anabaptist Vision and Mennonite Reality," *Consultation on Anabaptist Mennonite Theology*, A. J. Klassen, ed., p. 27.

29. Niebuhr, *op. cit.*, p. 31.

30. Yoder, *op. cit.*, p. 17.

Chapter 4: Christian Faith in Black and White

1. Preston N. Williams, "Ethnic Pluralism or Black Separatism," in *The White Problem* (Philadelphia: The United Presbyterian Church U.S.A., Office of Church and Society), p. 37.

2. Dixon and Foster, *op. cit.*, p. 47.

3. *Ibid.*, p. 26.

4. Margaret Walker, "Religion, Poetry, and History: Foundations for a New Educational System," Floyd B. Barbour, ed., *Black Seventies* (Boston: Sargent), pp. 286, 287.

5. Dixon and Foster, *op. cit.*, p. 26. See footnote.

6. *Ibid.*, p. 64.

7. *Ibid.*, p. 68.

8. *Ibid.*, p. 66.

9. *Ibid.*, p. 48.

10. A quote copied from an unknown source.

11. Gustavo Gutierrez, *A Theology of Liberation* (Maryknoll, N.Y.: Orbis Books, 1972), p. 11.

12. Joseph Barndt, *Liberating Our White Ghetto* (Minneapolis: Augsburg, 1972) p. 25.

13. *Ibid.*, p. 26.

14. Among some of the Latin American theologians I refer to are Rubem Alves, Gustavo Gutierrez, and Paulo Freire.

15. John J. Vincent, "A Renaissance for Theology through Racism," p. 1. He quotes Albert Cleage, Jr., *The Black Messiah* (Mission, Kan.: Sheed and Ward, 1969).

16. Cone, *Black Theology and Black Power, op. cit.*, p. 70.

17. *Ibid.*, p. 65.

A BLACK THEOLOGY BIBLIOGRAPHY

BOOKS

Baldwin, James. *The Fire Next Time*. New York: Dell Publishing Co., 1962.

Barbour, Floyd B., Ed., *The Black Power Revolt*, Boston: Extending Horizons Books, 1968.

Behm, Ronald and Columbus, Salley. *Your God Is Too White*. Downers Grove, Ill.: Inter-Varsity Press, 1970.

Cleage, Albert B., Jr. *The Black Messiah*. New York: Sheed and Ward, Inc. 1969.

Cone, James H. *Black Theology and Black Power* New York: Seabury Press, 1969.

———————. *A Black Theology of Liberation*. New York: Lippincott, 1970.

Frazier, Franklin, *The Negro Church in America*. New York: Schoken Books, 1963.

Gardiner, James, and Roberts, J. Deotis. *Quest for a Black Theology*. Philadelphia: Pilgrim Press, 1971.

Harding, Vincent. *Must Walls Divide*. New York: Friendship Press, 1965.

Johnson, Joseph A., Jr., *The Soul of the Black Preacher*. Philadelphia: United Church Press, 1971.

Jones, Major J. *Black Awareness: A Theology of Hope*. New York: Abingdon Press, 1971.

King, Martin Luther, Jr., *The Trumpet of Conscience*, New York: Harper and Row, 1968.

———————. *Where Do We Go from Here: Chaos or Community*. Boston: Beacon Press, 1968.

Marty, Martin E. and Peerman, Dean G., editors. *New Theology*. No. 6, New York: Macmillan, 1969.

———————. *New Theology*. No. 9, New York: Macmillan, 1972.

Mays, Benjamin E. *The Negro's God as Reflected in His Literature.* New York: Atheneum, 1969.

Roberts, J. Deotis, *Liberation and Reconciliation: A Black Theology.* Philadelphia: Westminster Press, 1971.

Schuchter, Arnold. *Reparations. The Black Manifesto and Its Challenge to White America.* Philadelphia: Lippincott, 1970.

Skinner, Tom. *How Black Is The Gospel.* Philadelphia: Lippincott, 1970.

Smith, Elwyn, ed. *What the Religious Revolutionaries Are Saying.* Philadelphia: Fortress Press, 1971.

Sontag, Frederick, and Roth, John K. *The American Religious Experience.* New York: Harper and Row, 1972.

Washington, Joseph R. *Black and White Power Subreption.* Boston: Beacon Press, 1969.

Washington, Joseph, Jr. *The Politics of God.* Boston: Beacon Press, 1967.

Wilmore, Gayraud S. *Black Religion and Black Radicalism.* New York: Doubleday and Co., 1970.

ARTICLES

"An Introduction to Black Theology." *Enquiry*, March-May, 1971.

Belm, Ron. "The Bible and Black Theology." *His Magazine*, March 1970.

Chapman, Clarke G. "American Theology in Black: James H. Cone." *Cross Currents*, Vol. XXII, Spring, 1972.

Cone, James. "Black Theology and Black Liberation." *Christian Century*, September 16, 1970.

——————— "Toward a Black Theology." *Ebony Magazine*, August 1970.

Cutler, Donald R. "The Religion of Black Power." *The Religious Situation*, Boston: Beacon Press, 1968.

Dickinson, Richard. "Black Theology and Black Power." *Encounter*, Autumn, 1970.

Duke, Robert W. "Black Theology and the Experience of Blackness." *The Journal of Religious Thought*, Vol. XXIX, Spring-Summer, 1972.

Gelzer, David G. "Random Notes on Black Theology and African Theology." *Christian Century*, September 16, 1970.

Hanson, Geddes. "Black Theology and Protestant Thought." *Social Progress*, September-October, 1969.

Harding, Vincent. "The Afro-American Past." *Motive*, April 1, 1968.

_____. "The American Christ and Black Power." *The Black Power Revolt*, 1968.

_____. "Reflections and Meditations on the Training of Religious Leaders for the New Black Generation." *Theological Education*, Spring, 1970.

_____. "The Religion of Black Power." *The Religious Situation*, Donald R. Culter, ed. Beacon Press, Boston, 1969.

Herzog, Frederick. "God: Black or White." *Review and Expositor*, Summer, 1970.

Hill, Bob. "The Dilemma of the Black Christian." *Moody Monthly*, September 1969.

Hodges, William. "Not by White Might or Black Power." *Christianity Today*, October 9, 1970.

Horton, Frank L. "Teaching Black History in the Local Church." *Christian Advocate*, February 5, 1970.

Johnson, Joseph A. "The Legitimacy of Black Theology." *Christian Index*, April 9, 1970.

Johnson, William R. "A Black Prayer and Litany." *Theology Today*, October 1969.

Jones, Lawrence N. "Black Churches in Historical Perspective." *Christianity and Crisis*, November 2 and 16, 1970.

Jones, Miles J. "Toward a Theology of the Black Experience." *Christian Century*, September 16, 1970.

Jones, William. "Theodicy and Methodology in Black Theology: A Critique of Washington, Cone, and Cleage." *Harvard Theological Review*, October 1971.

Kennedy, Robert F. "Suppose God Is Black." *Look*, August 23, 1966.

Kilmore, Thomas. "The Black Church." *Ebony*, August 1970.

Long, Charles H. "The Black Reality: Toward a Theology of Freedom." *Criterion*, 1969.

McClain, William. "The Genius of the Black Church." *Christianity and Crisis*, 1970.

Macquamie, John. "Liberal and Radical Theology." *The Modern Churchmen*, Vol. XV, No. 4, July 1972.

Powell, John H. "Toward a Unified Black Theology." Unpublished paper, 1972.

Roberts, J. Deotis. "African Religion and Social Consciousness," *The Journal of Religious Thought*, Vol. XXIX, Spring-Summer, 1972.

_____. "The Black Caucus and the Failure of Christian Theology." *The Journal of Religious Thought*, Vol. XXXVI, Summer, 1969.

_____ . "Black Theology and the Theological Revolution." *The Journal of Religious Thought*, Vol. XXVIII, Summer, 1971.

Rodgers, Cornish. "A New Theology for a New People." *Christian Century*, September 16, 1970.

Ruether, Rosemary Radford. "Outline for a Theology of Liberation," *DIALOG, A Journal of Theology*, Vol. II, Autumn, 1972.

Vincent, John J. "A Renaissance for Theology Through Racism," a paper.

Williams, Preston N. "Black Experience and Black Religion." *Theology Today*, October 1969.

_____ . "The Ethical Aspects of the Black Church/Black Theology," *The Journal of Religious Thought*, Vol. XXVIII, Spring-Summer, 1971.

_____ . "Ethics and Ethos of the Black Experience." *Christianity and Crisis*, May 1971.

Williams, Roger. "A Black Pastor Looks at Black Theology." *Harvard Theological Review*, 1971.

PAMPHLETS

Racism in America and How to Combat It. The United States Commission on Civil Rights. Clearing House Publication, January 1970.

The White Problem. Philadelphia: The United Presbyterian Church U.S.A., Office of Church and Society.

THE JOHN F. FUNK LECTURES

Black and Mennonite is the latest of a series of pamphlets and books which have resulted from John F. Funk Lectures. The Funk Lectures are commissioned by the Conrad Grebel Projects Committee and are financed by funds accumulated from royalties earned by Conrad Grebel Lecture books. The Funk Lectures published so far are as follows:

1. *The Christian Calling* (1961), by Virgil Vogt.
2. *Brotherhood and Schism* (1963), by Calvin Redekop.
3. *The Call to Preach* (1963), by Clayton Beyler.
4. *The Church Functions with Purpose* (1967), by Calvin Redekop.
5. *Demons: An Examination of Demons at Work in the World Today* (1972), by Donald R. Jacobs.
6. *Making Political Decisions* (1972), by John R. Redekop.
7. *Black and Mennonite: A Search for Identity* (1976), by Hubert L. Brown.

HUBERT L. BROWN, born at Norristown, Pennsylvania, is executive secretary of Mennonite Student Services for the Mennonite Board of Missions, Elkhart, Indiana.

He was pastor of Bethel Mennonite Church, Norristown, Pennsylvania, for two years, and of Spencer Mennonite Church, Swanton, Ohio, for three years.

He has served as chairman of the Home Missions Committee of the Mennonite Board of Missions and as an executive member of the Minority Ministries Council of the Mennonite Church.

He received his AA degree from Penn Wesleyan College, Allentown, Pennsylvania; his BA degree in English from Goshen College, Goshen, Indiana; and MEd degree from Indiana University, Bloomington, Indiana. He has studied at Associated Mennonite Biblical Seminaries, Elkhart, Indiana, and is pursuing a doctorate degree in education at Ball State University, Muncie, Indiana.

Brown has worked as counselor at Indiana University and as director of the Elkhart Urban League, Elkhart, Indiana. He is a member of the Mennonite Historical Committee, the Commission on Congregational Leadership, the Mennonite Board of Congregational Ministries, a task force on minority leadership for Goshen Biblical Seminary, and a group studying the needs of minority students at Goshen College.

Brown is author of two volumes of poetry, *Black Coffee* and *Through the Smoke Holes* published by Pinchpenny Press, Goshen, Indiana. His articles have appeared in *Gospel Herald*, *With*, and college newspapers.

He holds membership in the Association for the Coordination of University Religious Affairs, the American Personnel and Guidance Association, and is on the board of directors of Ministries to Blacks in Higher Education.

He is married to Helen Reichel Brown and is the father of two children, Leslie and Donald. He resides with his family in Elkhart, Indiana, and is a member of the South Side Fellowship.

Made in the USA
Middletown, DE
19 July 2015